CW00666523

I have read books on how to make
have read books on how to make s
but this book wants your sermon
this little book mandatory readi
then urge them to read it a couple
ministry. It avoids cutesy and manipulative suggestions, and makes its
practical points while urging integrity, faithfulness, and imagination.
Many books on preaching are published every year; this one is a 'must'.

DA Carson
Research Professor of New Testament
Trinity Evangelical Divinity School, Chicago, Illinois

Some writing so solemnly exalts the task of preaching, or so heavily
complicates the method, it depresses and discourages ordinary mortals
like me into thinking *we* can never really do it and should just give up.
Since most preachers feel that every Sunday night anyway, such books
don't really help the cause! This one does. I like it because it is short,
lighthearted (but not lightweight), very human, and very much to the
point. I am involved in training preachers, but I still have plenty to
learn. I am very grateful for a resource that will both help me, and help
me in helping others—with enjoyment, encouragement and some fun
along the way!

William JU Philip
Senior Minister
The Tron Church, Glasgow

Let me invite you to eavesdrop on an Irish-Aussie conversation about
preaching. This book teems with 'plusses': it is *short* (as a tome that
takes Eutychus as its poster boy must be); it is *stretching* (the authors
force one to deal with longer texts—and leave one asking, "Why can't
I summarize extended passages like that?"); it is *specific* (they include
actual sermons with critique); it is *searching* (in case you skip the first
chapter, 'pray' occurs eight times in the conclusion); and *stirring* (you
still want to preach when you've finished reading). If you don't buy the
book, don't cry if Eutychus isn't saved!

Dale Ralph Davis
Author and Bible expositor
Cookeville, Tennessee

The late Klaas Runia entitled his Moore College lectures of 1980 *The Sermon Under Attack*. The only thing new about the current attack on expository preaching is that which it nominates to be its substitute—these days, it's narrative or storytelling. But the people of God know that the Bible preached, explained to the mind, applied to the will, is precisely the nourishment they need, and which alone promotes their maturity.

I am very pleased to recommend this book by Phil and Gary, two faithful expositors. Our old friend Chappo, to whom it is dedicated, would be pleased as well. I can hear him saying, "Get to the text brother! The authority is in the text. Tell them what the text says, and do it in 20 minutes." We are grateful for Chappo's ministry and grateful to our brothers by extending its emphasis through this book.

David Cook
Former Principal
Sydney Missionary and Bible College, NSW

I needed to read this book by Campbell and Millar at this point in my life. I've been preaching for over 27 years, and this book has convicted me of fundamentals that have ceased to be central in my preaching.

Every preacher needs to read this book every five years. It is both theologically driven and brimming with wise and practical insights on how to preach.

Ray Galea
Senior Minister
St Alban's Multicultural Bible Ministry, Sydney, NSW

Worried your preaching, though of course biblical, may be getting a bit jaded, even boring? This humdinger of a book is just for you: full of marvellous insights from areas as diverse as biblical theology, preaching the Old Testament, and mode of delivery; and written like the sermons it is encouraging us to preach—faithful but fresh. A must-read, a short read, a great read, for preachers at every stage, whether young colt or old nag. Buy, read, apply!

John Samuel
Senior Minister
Duke Street Church, Richmond, Surrey

Millar and Campbell write with much wit and wisdom for the sake of our listeners. At some point every preacher must decide whether to preach for the regard of one's peers or for the welfare of Christ's people. Millar and Campbell have obviously decided for the latter and give much sound advice for the rest of us to do the same.

Bryan Chapell
Chancellor
Covenant Theological Seminary, St Louis, Missouri

Two men who would never be deadly boring or dull are Gary Millar and Phil Campbell, and in this book they use their lively wit to help other preachers keep Eutychus awake. More importantly, they are united in their understanding of and commitment to the task of making God's word known. I pray this book will be of benefit to both preachers and congregations.

Phillip D Jensen
Dean of Sydney
St Andrew's Cathedral, Sydney, NSW

This book fills a gap in our concern for better preaching because it joins true piety to good theology in a way that few books do. Gary and Phil bring lots of experience, wisdom and practicality to the most privileged job in the universe—handling the word of God. It's a short, sharp and wonderfully honest Irish/Aussie injection.

Simon Manchester
Senior Minister
St Thomas' Anglican Church, North Sydney, NSW

This book deserves to be included in the 'must read' category for preachers. It is readable, which always helps! And, as we would expect, it is biblical and practical. But it is also funny and forthright in a way that made me re-evaluate my preaching and resolve with God's help to improve. This is a different book from Lloyd-Jones' *Preaching and Preachers* and *Between Two Worlds* by John Stott, but it may prove to be just as influential.

Alistair Begg
Senior Pastor
Parkside Church, Cleveland, Ohio

To Fiona and Louise, who have helped us more
with our preaching than anyone else, and with
grateful thanks to Chappo (1930-2012).

Saving Eutychus

How to preach God's word
and keep people awake

Gary Millar and
Phil Campbell

Saving Eutychus
© Matthias Media 2013

Matthias Media
(St Matthias Press Ltd ACN 067 558 365)
PO Box 225
Kingsford NSW 2032
Australia
Telephone: (02) 9233 4627; international: +61 2 9233 4627
Email: info@matthiasmedia.com.au
Internet: www.matthiasmedia.com.au

Matthias Media (USA)
Telephone: 330 953 1702; international: +1 330 953 1702
Email: sales@matthiasmedia.com
Internet: www.matthiasmedia.com

ISBN 978 1 922206 25 1

Cover design and typesetting by Lankshear Design.

Paul spoke to the people and, because he intended to leave the next day, kept on talking until midnight... Seated in a window was a young man named Eutychus, who was sinking into a deep sleep as Paul talked on and on. When he was sound asleep, he fell to the ground from the third story...

Splattttt.

Acts 20:7, 9 (NIV)

Contents

An Aussie and an Irishman walk into a pulpit...

PREACHING IS HARD WORK. And—we're sorry to break this to you if you're just starting out—it doesn't seem to get much easier. But God in his kindness gives us people to encourage us that we're on the right track, to sharpen us and to help us to keep going. That's how an Aussie and a Northern Irishman ended up writing a book on preaching together.

We have very different backgrounds, personalities and experience. We have very different interests and passions. Our families are at very different stages. And as you will discover in this book, we express ourselves differently and approach preaching from different angles. But those differences are part of what has led to this book. From the moment we met in 2010, we recognized that we had independently come to many of the same key convictions about teaching the Bible.

While the details of our processes will vary, we are both completely committed to teaching the Bible book by book in a way that is faithful and fresh. And we share the same concern for saving Eutychus—preaching should never bore people to death. We both look for the 'big idea' that unifies the passage we're preaching on, and we both tend to preach on longer 'chunks' of text, as defined by the underlying movement of these big ideas. For both of us, preaching begins with God speaking, moving, thrilling, teaching, correcting and wooing us through a passage of the Bible. As God's truth begins to sink into our own hearts and lives, God enables us to think more clearly and deeply about its application in the lives of those to whom we're speaking. This is the process, in a nutshell, that we both follow and will be unpacking in the pages ahead: work out the big idea; apply it to ourselves; think through how to preach it.

It's interesting and stimulating, though, to think about the differences in our preaching as we work together. I (Gary) think Phil's style is crisper and shorter, and he's brilliant at reducing an argument to the bare minimum. I tend to take a little longer to get there, and (I think) I spend more time trying to work the text under our skin. These differences reflect, in part, who we are (an Aussie and an Irishman), our theological influences, our personalities (for Phil the glass is usually half-empty, and for me it's at least three-quarters full) and our personal convictions. But as flawed people and preachers, we are trying to do exactly the same thing. And what we want to do in the pages that follow is to encourage you to work harder on the biblical text, on the content of your sermon and on your delivery, so that you continue to grow as the preacher that only you can be. Our prayer is that this book will equip and encourage you to preach the word of God in a way that fits your own personality and is faithful and fresh in your own context.

There are key elements of sermon preparation and delivery that all of us need to learn and practise. There are other aspects that are a matter of personal preference and style. We're aware that some of the things we're suggesting here reflect who we are and where we've been. We both have unfortunate quirks that we couldn't unlearn even if we wanted to, as well as many things we're still learning to improve. We're far from being 'perfect preachers'—yet along the way we have grown and changed. We hope that hearing our two voices and learning from our experiences will help you gain confidence in your own 'voice' and see some fresh ways in which you can continue to develop as a preacher too.

In the chapters that follow we are both very open about the way God has worked in us over the years. You will have multiple glimpses into our lives and families, so it may help you to know a little bit about us up front.

I was born in Northern Ireland, am married to Fiona (a Scot born in Peru), and have three daughters—Lucy (11), Sophie (10) and Rebekah (6). We moved to Australia at the start of 2011, where I am the Principal of Queensland Theological College (QTC) in Brisbane. Before that, I was minister of Howth and Malahide Presbyterian Church in Dublin in the Republic of Ireland for 12 years (and was on the staff of a large church in Northern Ireland before that). I studied chemistry in Belfast, and then theology in Aberdeen, before completing a DPhil at Oxford (on Deuteronomy).

Phil and Louise are the parents of four adult children—Nathan, Jo, Maddie and Susie—and they are now learning the art of grandparenting (even though they insist they're much too young). Nathan's popular blog www.st-eutychus.com inspired the title of this book.

Phil leads the ministry team at Mitchelton Presbyterian Church on Brisbane's north side and, as past chair of QTC, he helped persuade Gary to move his family halfway around the world. For over a decade, Phil has also loved teaching the introductory preaching course at QTC, and much of the material in this book has been road tested there.

One thing we do have in common is that our respective wives, Fiona and Louise, have taught us more about preaching and been a greater help to us than anyone else. Not only is this book written *for* them, it would probably also have been much better if it had been written *by* them.

A host of people along the way have also helped us a great deal. In addition to those who have graciously listened to us teach the Bible in our churches over the years, various mentors and friends have journeyed with us, sharpening and encouraging us along the way. For me, these people include Bob Lockhart, William Still, Warner Hardie, Dave Mansfield, John Chapman, colleagues at the Irish Preachers Conference and the Dublin Gospel Partnership, Nigel McCullough and, above all, my closest friends Andrew Smith (whose wife Tara has worked miracles in making a book out of our material) and David 'Monty' Montgomery. For Phil, these people include Donald Campbell, Phillip Jensen, David Cook, John Chapman, Bryson Smith (who models all the ideas in this book brilliantly) and the members of the Pearl Beach Preaching Group.

If you read through that list of names, you'll have noticed that we have one influence in common—Canon John Chapman. Until Chappo went to his reward a few weeks ago, he encouraged us and countless others like us to "know and tell the gospel" with the constant reminder that "the first 50 years are the hardest". Neither of us has been at it for 50 years yet, but Chappo's example keeps us going. Our hope is that this book is a fitting thank you to God for his life and ministry.

Gary Millar

Phil Campbell

Saving Eutychus

IT'S CROWDED IN THE upstairs room, and stuffy, so young Eutychus wedges himself onto a windowsill and sucks in the cool outside air. But fresh air isn't enough. The visiting preacher talks on and on. By midnight, Eutychus is asleep on his perch. His weight shifts, he tumbles... and moments later his body lies broken on the pavement three stories below (see Acts 20:7, 9).

The rest, as they say, is history—though happily, thanks to some apostolic first aid, the young man's 'terminal velocity' wasn't as *terminal* as it could have been.

Now, before we unjustly judge the preacher here, let's consider the extenuating circumstances. Paul had arrived in Troas on his whistlestop tour of the Aegean to proclaim the kingdom of God, and time was short. The night Eutychus struggled to stay awake was Paul's last among them, and there was a lot he wanted to teach them. Paul couldn't catch a later flight and prolong his stay; he had to keep talking. But the humbling point we want to make is that what took Paul many hours of speaking to achieve—near-fatal napping—takes most of us only a few minutes speaking to a well-rested and caffeinated crowd on a Sunday.

So why does Luke include this story in Acts 20? Is it proof that some people would rather die than listen to an overlong sermon? Or maybe it's a warning to preachers—if you lack Paul's apostolic healing gifts, keep people awake at all costs.

How are you doing with that? I try hard to avoid being dull, yet most weeks I find myself losing one or two over the edge. When I met the doctor who was about to sedate me for an endoscopy, I couldn't help joking, "Hi Doc, I see we're both in the business of putting people to sleep! Call me next time you've got a tough case." But it's not all that funny. And the difference between us (apart from a lower hourly rate) is that I *don't want* to be in the business of putting people to sleep.

Gary and I are not approaching this book as experts on preaching that keeps people awake. But we are convinced that when attention wanders and eyes droop, it's more often our fault than our listeners'. It's our job to keep people awake, and we'll take the blame if they fall out the window. But if you've just resolved to learn a new stand-up routine for Sunday, hold on. Our challenge is not just to avoid being deadly dull. Our challenge is also to be faithful, accurate and clear as we cut to the heart of the biblical text and apply what God is *really saying* in a way that cuts to the hearts of people who are *really listening*.

When Bill Hybels visited Sydney in the early 1990s, Australian evangelist John Chapman ('Chappo') was in the audience. Most of us found Bill's talk on Matthew the tax collector riveting, and as best as I can remember it included plenty of practical party tips, given the fact that the tax collector threw a massive Jesus-party and invited all his friends.

When Bill invited questions, Chappo raised his hand. "Dear brother", said Chappo, "I'm not meaning to be rude, but I wonder if you could tell us how people are to know when they are hearing God speak through his word, and when they are just hearing good advice from Bill? Because as far as I could tell, I couldn't spot the difference. As you spoke to us, it all seemed to come with the same authority."

Chappo had a point. Hybels had sanctified a bunch of commonsense suggestions by mixing them with the text of Luke 5 and delivering them with all the authority of Scripture. None of it was wrong. It was just that none of his points were the points Luke was actually making. Sure, Luke *mentioned* the party—but he wasn't telling us to have one. It wasn't God speaking. It was Bill.

Saving Eutychus doesn't just mean keeping him awake. It also means doing our best to keep him fresh and alert so he can hear the truth of the gospel and be saved. If we have done our job, we will stand up on Sunday ready to deliver a sermon on a Bible passage that we have wrestled with and that the Holy Spirit has begun to apply to our own hearts and lives. We will know exactly what we want to say and how we're going to say it in a fresh and engaging way. We will have prayed for God to reach the hearts of our listeners with his word. When that's happening, snoring is not an option. None of this, however, can happen without prayer.

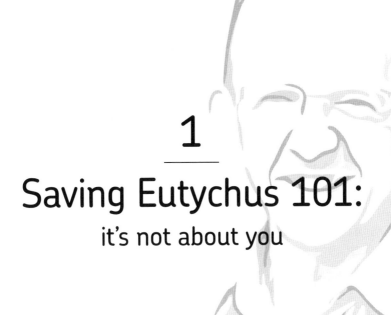

1

Saving Eutychus 101:

it's not about you

WRITING A BOOK ABOUT preaching makes me very uncomfortable. I know there are all kinds of dos and don'ts and useful tips and techniques. As we'll see, there are plenty of helpful things to say about biblical theology, and pace, and illustrations, and approach and so on. But my biggest fear in putting all this down on paper is that it makes it sound as if preaching is all about the preacher—what we say and how we say it. But it isn't.

Everyone who has ever preached regularly knows something about the mystery of the sermon that you thought was brilliantly constructed but fell completely flat. In God's kindness, you may also have listened to yourself giving a really dud sermon that led someone to become a Christian (I much prefer those days!). Why does that happen? It's because God works through preaching. And we really do need to remember that. That's why this chapter (which doesn't say anything particularly new but, like a good sermon, points us to the truth of which we need to be constantly reminded) may actually be the most important chapter in this entire book.

Praying in our generation

My guess is that people in almost every generation have thought that prayer was going out of fashion. "People are much more self-reliant than they used to be", our grandparents said. Then our parents said the same thing. And now you might be thinking it, too. I suppose it's part of living in a fallen world. But even so, I think that our generation, in the second decade of the 21st century, faces some particular challenges when it comes to encouraging God's people to keep praying.

When I was a student in Aberdeen in northern Scotland in the late 1980s, the main obstacle to getting out of bed in the morning to pray was the fact that it was freezing and the heating didn't work. Although living in Brisbane has greatly reduced the thermal challenges, 25 years later I face a whole new set of temptations every morning.

Now when I wake up in the morning not only would I rather stay in bed, but my phone is right there, calling me. I can check emails and sports scores from the northern hemisphere, read the news and even play Scrabble if the mood takes me. I can read my favourite blog posts, catch up on Zite, check the weather radar, look to see who's on Skype across the world. Or I could get up and pray. But even if I make it out of bed, the millions of potentially distracting details only a touch away continue to clamour for my attention. Facebook and

Twitter are just two of them. But even when I've successfully negotiated all of this, am fully awake, have a cup of coffee in my hand and am ready to concentrate, I've wasted at least 20 minutes and am feeling the pressure to 'get on' for Sunday. So what do I do? I start to read or write (rather than *pray*).

I know that the temptation to skip prayer for other 'more productive' activity is not new. It's just incredibly easy now— distractions are literally at our fingertips. And nowhere is that more obvious than when it comes to praying for (and before) preaching.

Prayer for preachers and preaching

It's strange but true that one of the consequences of having access to great teaching and great resources is a growing self-reliance (which I think is also a particular challenge for our generation).

Those of you under 40 may find it difficult to imagine that when I was a student minister, we had to go to a place called a 'library' to find information in 'books'. Occasionally, we were also able to get things called 'cassettes'. Since cassettes were (a) expensive, and (b) hard to get, they were passed around, used, re-used and abused. (In fact, I would still love to hear the end of the Martyn Lloyd-Jones talk on Romans 11 that someone recorded ABBA's *Greatest Hits* over!) Contrast that with today—a quick glance at the Gospel Coalition website gives instant access to thousands of excellent expository sermons. The issue today isn't lack of resources, but rather how 'ordinary' pastors compete for the listening ears of their congregations with the 'big guns', whose sermons are available live (or at least later on the same day they were preached).

There are, of course, many ways in which this is a good thing—I mean, seriously, can we ever have too much good teaching? And yet there are dangers. One of these is that teaching the Bible becomes completely detached from loving relationship. Another danger stems from the fact that people place far too much emphasis on the preacher as 'performer' (or even 'personality'). And when that happens, it effectively removes the need for prayer.

In the local church, if we are regularly rubbing shoulders with those who preach, we know that there are weeks when they are under huge pressure to carve out enough time to prepare properly; we know that there are weeks when they just can't nail their sermon; we know that there are weeks when their kids are playing up, or they are working through marital issues, or they are feeling under the weather. And so we pray. We know that our friends—those who have just received crushing health news, who have recently been bereaved, who are struggling with anger, who are trying to deal with pride, who have sinned sexually—will be listening to this sermon. We know how much we need God. And so we pray (or so we know we should). But if we are sitting in front of a screen watching or listening to an old sermon preached by a guy we don't know, in a place we've never been, to people we've never met, it isn't quite the same. To put it bluntly, it doesn't really matter to us if God showed up and addressed his people through his word that day. It doesn't really matter what was going on in that church. So why should we pray? The connection between our prayers and the sermon is broken— and when that happens, it isn't easily fixed.

Preachers praying

I could be wrong, but I strongly suspect that preachers are praying less today too. They (we) are certainly talking less about prayer than, say, 20 years ago. And while it's true that there has been a significant resurgence of biblical *preaching*, I'm not sure this has been accompanied by a resurgence in praying—and especially not prayer about preaching.

Gradually, we seem to be losing sight of the fact that God uses weak and sinful people, and that he uses them only by grace. Yes, we may sow, plant and water—but *only God* gives growth. That's true in your local church and mine. It's also true of every podcast and ebook and conference address under the sun. God doesn't use people because they are gifted. He uses people (even preachers) because he is gracious. Do we actually believe that? If we do believe it, then we will pray—we will pray before we speak, and we will pray for others before they speak. It's that simple.

Prayer and preaching in the Bible

In the book of Acts, it's hard to miss the fact that the apostles gave their attention "to prayer and to the ministry of the word" (Acts 6:4). But what does this actually mean? Up to this point in Acts, there hasn't been that much praying (so, for example, it isn't even completely clear whether 2:42 means 'they prayed' or 'they kept going to the temple'). But in Acts 4:24-30 we see that when the church prays, it prays for the preaching of the apostles. And although I can't prove it, I suspect that from this point on in Acts praying for the impact of the apostles' preaching is considered a complete no-brainer.

We can see basically the same concern when Paul writes to the Colossians:

> Continue steadfastly in prayer, being watchful in it with thanksgiving. At the same time, pray also for us, that God may open to us a door for the word, to declare the mystery of Christ, on account of which I

am in prison—that I may make it clear, which is how
I ought to speak. (Col 4:2)

Paul clearly expects—and longs for—the prayers of the
Christians at Colossae for his *preaching*.

So what should we do?

Let me give you a straightforward double challenge.

First, resolve to make sure that from now on (whatever
your habit has been in the past), you will pray for your own
preaching. Perhaps you have been totally consistent in this for
years. It may be that you would never dream of standing up
to speak to anyone without praying that God would help you
to believe and live your own sermon. And it may be that you
always pray for those on whom you are about to inflict the
sermon—if that's you, well and good. However, if you are part
of the (large?) number of Bible teachers who would be rather
embarrassed (or deeply ashamed?) if the amount of time and
energy they had put into praying through and for the sermon
were to be announced to the congregation just before they
stood up to speak, this may be a great time to hit the reset
button and repent.

The second part of the challenge is this: make sure that
your church prays *together* for the preaching. I haven't done
any exhaustive research (well, actually, I haven't done any
research at all on this), but I suspect that the church prayer
meeting is in rapid decline. The growth of home groups is, I
think, a really good thing, but it doesn't come without a cost.
In my experience, the cost is that the 'prayer' part of the home
group is *always* weaker than the study part. The net result is
that we pray more for my Aunt Nelly's next-door neighbour's
friend's daughter than we do for the proclamation of the

message of Jesus. (And it's not that my Aunt Nelly's next-door neighbour's friend's daughter doesn't need prayer—I'm arguing for both/and rather than either/or.) So, again, it's just worth checking—is there a dedicated time during the week when people gather specifically to pray for our core business? If not, please make one.

A final word: What this looks like in practice

I am, like all of us, a child of my past. And when it comes to prayer, I am very definitely a child of a particular part of my past. From 1988-1991 (when I was a theological student), I was part of a remarkable church family. Gilcomston South Church of Scotland in Aberdeen wasn't a huge church. Nor was it a particularly 'happening' church. We met twice on a Sunday, had a midweek central Bible study and a Saturday night prayer meeting—and that was it. There was an organ, and we sang five hymns or psalms (often to Germanic minor tunes). The pastor, William Still, preached steadily through the Bible (this was still relatively novel at the time, even though he had been doing it for 40 years). But what set that church family apart was its very simple commitment to "the ministry of the word nourished by prayer" (as Mr Still would repeatedly say). I have never been part of a church family that had a greater sense of expectancy when we gathered to hear the Bible explained. I have never been part of a church family where prayer was so obviously the heartbeat of everything that went on. And I have never been part of a church family where God was so obviously present week by week as he spoke through his word. And, it seems to me, there might just be a connection.

Of course 'Gilc' was, and is, just like any church family—full of flawed, messed-up people like you and me. But those of us who had the privilege of 'passing through' went on from there with an indelible sense that preaching and praying go together. It was just part of the DNA of the church family. The precious group of 50 or 60 people who met week by week at the Saturday night prayer meeting spent most of the two hours praying for the proclamation of the gospel elsewhere—in other churches in their city, in Scotland, and on every continent around the world, one by one. Eventually, someone would pray, "And Lord, spare a thought for us in our own place tomorrow…" and the others, who had been praying faithfully on their own all through the week for the preaching at Gilc, would murmur a heartfelt "Amen".

2
Preaching that changes the heart

WE ALL KNOW GOOD preaching when we hear it. We may not be able to explain why it is so good. We may not know why the sermon enthralled and challenged us this Sunday, or why this time last week we were counting the bricks in the wall behind the pulpit. But we know there *is* a difference, and all of us can feel that difference.

I hope you've heard the Bible taught in such a way that you simply could not miss the fact that God was in the room addressing his people through his word. I hope you've felt that strange combination of fear and comfort as you suspect that the preacher wrote the sermon just for you (and as you wonder whether the speaker has been secretly interviewing your parents, spouse, children, workmates and neighbours again). That's the kind of preaching that changes the heart, and that's the kind of preaching we want to explore in this chapter.

Of course, some of the impact we're talking about is purely the result of the Holy Spirit working through flawed people in a way that is dramatic, unpredictable and basically miraculous. And while we can and must pray for God to work in that way in the hearts of our listeners (as we've just seen in chapter 1), another part of our job as preachers is to aim for that impact as we think, write and preach.

The aim of this book is to help us all to preach in a way that is faithful to Scripture without being dull. Some of the steps we need to take to achieve this are spiritual, some are technical, and some are theological. In this chapter, we're going to take a look at an area where these three concerns overlap. We're going to explore what we call preaching to the heart.

Preaching that changes the heart—what it is and why it matters

If I had to choose one statement that has shaped my convictions about preaching and that encapsulates what I long to see happen when I preach, it would be this from Jonathan Edwards:

> If true religion lies much in the affections we may infer that such means are to be desired as have much tendency to move the affections. Such books, and such a way of preaching the word and the administration of the ordinances, and such a way of worshipping God in prayer and praises, as has a tendency deeply

to affect the hearts of those who attend these means, is much to be desired.[1]

When Edwards uses the word 'affections' here, he isn't talking primarily about the emotions. He uses the word 'heart' here in the Old Testament sense of 'control centre of the personality', which is really a shorthand way of saying 'the essential me'. Edwards longs for Bible teaching that affects the way we think and feel and act. He wants his sermons to move people and result in real and lasting change. He wants to preach in a way that, under God, changes people's hearts. And don't we all?

When you listen to someone explain the Bible, what do you want to get out of it? I want to know that God has addressed me through his word. I want to be challenged, humbled, corrected, excited, moved, strengthened, overawed, corrected, shaped, stretched and propelled out into the world as a different person. I want to be changed! And if I'm the one who's teaching the Bible—whether it's to my children, to our students in college, to our church family in Brisbane, or to anybody else—I long for that change to happen in the hearts of those who hear. I long for Jane to find new security in Christ, and for Rob to discover real joy in following Jesus. I want Ian to stop doing that because he realizes it is dishonouring God, and I want everyone to be bowled over by the power and beauty of God. I want people (myself included) to become more like Christ. To borrow Edwards' language, I want people to be affected. I want to preach in a way that results in change. Real change. Heart change.

1   J Edwards, *Treatise on the Religious Affections*, IVP, Leicester, 1974, p. 35.

What's the difference between preaching to the heart and manipulation?

Preaching that changes the heart is incredibly powerful. And many of us, I suspect, start to get a bit edgy when we talk about power and transforming change. Because while of course we want God to change people through his word, we are very nervous about manipulating people. And so we should be. The New Testament is full of warnings against people who have an agenda, and commends a straightforward approach to sharing the message of the gospel. So, for example, 2 Corinthians 4:2 says:

> But we have renounced disgraceful, underhanded ways. We refuse to practise cunning or to tamper with God's word, but by the open statement of the truth we would commend ourselves to everyone's conscience in the sight of God.

Paul urges us to make it impossible for people to dismiss us as hucksters by concentrating on the open statement of the truth. He says, "No tricks!" But doesn't that undermine the whole rationale for this book? No, it doesn't. And here's why.

The opposite of practising cunning or tampering with the truth is not being faithful but dull. Rather, it is being so truth-driven that we wouldn't dream of twisting the message to suit our own ends or of trying to manipulate either the message or people to promote our own agenda. But that doesn't exclude trying to present the truth in a way that maximizes its impact. Paul's exhortation to state the truth openly and plainly, properly understood, should drive us to explain the text in a way that connects with people at a deep level—or to put it slightly differently, to preach in a way that changes people's hearts.

On the one hand, we want to speak plainly and avoid being sly or underhanded. But on the other, because we long for people to be changed through our Bible teaching, we don't want to speak so plainly that what we say comes across as dull. Neither do we want to try to produce results by implementing a few slick techniques. It's a fine line, isn't it?

Interestingly, Paul himself feels the same tension. You can see it, for example, in Galatians 4:16-19:

> Have I then become your enemy by telling you the truth? They make much of you, but for no good purpose. They want to shut you out, that you may make much of them [that's manipulation]. It is always good to be made much of for a good purpose, and not only when I am present with you, my little children, for whom I am again in the anguish of childbirth until Christ is formed in you [that's godly concern]!

So how do we strike that balance of avoiding manipulation and making sure that our preaching isn't simply blandly conveying information? I think we find the answer to this question in that little phrase Paul uses in 2 Corinthians 4. He says we are to commit ourselves to "the open statement of the truth". But 'open statement' is a bit weak here. The Greek word he uses, according to Louw and Nida, means "to cause something to be fully known by revealing clearly and in some detail—'to make known, to make plain, to reveal, to bring to the light, to disclose, revelation'".[2] The key to preaching, then, is to make the message of the text obvious. Help people to see it and feel it. Help people to *understand* the text. Paul is talking about what I would call 'expository preaching', in which the message of the text is the message of the sermon.

---

2   JP Louw and EA Nida, *Greek-English Lexicon of the New Testament,* 2nd edn, vol. 1, United Bible Societies, London, 1999, pp. 338-9.

I am utterly convinced that the kind of preaching that changes people's lives, that changes people's hearts, is preaching that allows the text to speak. And I'm also convinced that this is exactly what the Bible itself does.

The long pedigree (and many faces) of preaching to the heart

The Scottish theologian PT Forsyth said:

> The great reason why the preacher must return continually to the Bible is that the Bible is the greatest sermon in the world. Above every other function of it the Bible is a sermon, a *kerugma*, a preachment. It is the preacher's book because it is the preaching book.[3]

This insight is vital. If the Bible 'preaches' (and clearly it does), then that should surely shape the way we preach.

Charles Spurgeon, the great 19th-century Baptist preacher, repeatedly said that we need to defend the Bible about as much as we need to defend a lion. A much better strategy is to let it loose. When we teach the Bible, our goal or aim should always be to 'uncage the lion'. I think that's what Paul is talking about when he uses that little phrase "the open statement of the truth". He is talking about enabling people to feel the impact of the text; he is talking about helping people to hear what God is saying in the text.

Where God is explaining something, we need to help people to understand. Where God is warning us, we need to help people feel the urgency and weight of that. Where God is wooing us, we need to help people feel the pull of his love.

---

3 PT Forsyth, *Positive Preaching and Modern Mind,* Kessinger Publishing, Whitefish, 2003, p. 10. By the way, 'preachment' is a sadly neglected Scottish word for a sermon!

Where God is correcting us, we need to show people that they are going the wrong way and to help them get back on track. Where God is comforting his people, we want people to feel the security and warmth of his comfort. And that, in a nutshell, is expository preaching.

Expository preaching happens when the message of the text = the message of the sermon. Or perhaps better, expository preaching happens when the vibe of the passage = the vibe of the sermon. While that may appear to be self-evident (isn't a sermon about a particular passage always going to have as its message the message of the passage?), unfortunately that's not always the case. And so there's an important distinction to be made here. Preaching involves conveying information, of course, but it is more than that. The 'message' of a passage is often not simply propositional—the purpose of a passage, for example, may not be simply to convey the information that our situation without Christ is bad. God may have given us this part of the Bible to make us *feel* bad (or joyful, or foolish, or repentant). As Kevin Vanhoozer helpfully points out, "Not only our minds, but also our emotional responses are brought under scriptural authority".[4]

So, for example, the sermon I heard many years ago about the 'five stones' David used to kill Goliath may have said some helpful things about faith, prayer, courage and so on, but it missed the point that "the battle is the LORD's" (1 Sam 17:47). Similarly, a sermon on David and Jonathan's relationship that praises human friendship but doesn't mention the fact that *Jonathan could have reasonably expected to be the next king but submits to David as the Lord's 'anointed'* may say some worthwhile things but has not picked up the 'vibe' of the passage as a whole.

---

4 KJ Vanhoozer, 'The Semantics of Biblical Literature', in DA Carson and JD Woodbridge (eds), *Hermeneutics, Authority, and Canon,* IVP, Downers Grove, 1986, pp. 53-104.

Our contention is that the Bible itself preaches to the heart. Through a huge range of genres across the sweep of biblical history, through the voices of known and unknown authors, God speaks to move and change people.

Expository preaching, then, isn't simply one technique or approach amongst many; it's the model that allows Scripture to speak most clearly and powerfully. The key to preaching in a way that affects people's hearts is to let the text speak in all its richness and variety. When we do that, what Vanhoozer calls the "illocutionary effect" of Scripture is at the forefront. Vanhoozer helpfully shows that God's words do more than simply convey information—they bring about results. They drive us to repentance, strengthen us, expose guilt, move us to gasp, and so on. And so our focus rests firmly on God doing his work through his word.

It would, of course, be overstating the case to say that other ways of teaching the Bible that pay less attention to context, literary genre, and the sweep of the Bible completely eradicate the "illocutionary effect". Regardless of how we teach the Bible, God can always achieve the effect for which the Scriptures were written. However, it is also clear that only when the Scriptures are allowed to set the agenda—only when the message (or vibe) of the sermon = the message (or vibe) of the text—is this effect most evident. Preaching that changes the heart, then, is simply preaching that allows the words of God to speak.

There is, of course, nothing new in this approach. Luther once said of the Reformation, "I simply taught, preached, and wrote God's Word... And while I slept, or drank Wittenberg beer with my friends... the Word did it all."[5] Calvin was, at

---

5   M Luther, 'Second Sermon on Monday after Invocavit, March 10, 1522', in JW Doberstein and HT Lehmann (eds), *Luther's Works*, vol. 51, Fortress Press, Philadelphia, 1958, p. 75.

one stage, exiled from Geneva for a period of several years. When he left, he was in the middle of a series of sermons preaching through the Bible. When he came back, he stood up the next morning and started to explain the very next verse. This is what the Reformers did. They didn't see themselves as doing anything new, but rather recovering the practice of the early church. But it isn't simply the fact that this approach has a long pedigree that commends it. A more compelling argument is simply that in the Bible itself, allowing the words of God to speak is the consistent pattern of effecting change in the human heart. Let's look at how that works in four key passages—two in the Old Testament and two in the New.

(i) Deuteronomy 4:32-40

"For ask now of the days that are past, which were before you, since the day that God created man on the earth, and ask from one end of heaven to the other, whether such a great thing as this has ever happened or was ever heard of. Did any people ever hear the voice of a god speaking out of the midst of the fire, as you have heard, and still live? Or has any god ever attempted to go and take a nation for himself from the midst of another nation, by trials, by signs, by wonders, and by war, by a mighty hand and an outstretched arm, and by great deeds of terror, all of which the LORD your God did for you in Egypt before your eyes? To you it was shown, that you might know that the LORD is God; there is no other besides him. Out of heaven he let you hear his voice, that he might discipline you. And on earth he let you see his great fire, and you heard his words out of the midst of the fire. And because he loved your fathers and chose their offspring after them and brought you out of Egypt with his own presence, by his great power, driving out before you nations greater and mightier than you, to bring you in, to give you their land for an inheritance, as it is this day, know therefore today, and lay it to your heart, that the LORD is God in heaven above and on the earth beneath; there is no other. Therefore you shall keep his statutes and his commandments, which I command you today, that it may go well with you and with your children after you, and that you may prolong your days in the land that the LORD your God is giving you for all time."

In Deuteronomy 4, Moses is explaining the significance and long-term impact of the events that took place 40 years before at Mount Sinai. This is a definitive moment in God's unfolding plan. This is the moment when God 'gathers' his people to speak to them. You could say that this is the moment when the 'church', the 'gathering of God', begins. And what happens? God speaks. And he speaks to discipline his people. He speaks to change them, to shape them. The Hebrew word for that is *yasar*, and it implies an action that leads to correction or improvement. When God speaks, his words have a powerful impact on his people.

The final verse above implies that God's word has the power to change his people, but verses 3-6 in chapter 6 make this explicit:

"Hear [listen] therefore, O Israel, and be careful to do them, that it may go well with you, and that you may multiply greatly, as the LORD, the God of your fathers, has promised you, in a land flowing with milk and honey.

"Hear [listen], O Israel: The LORD our God, the

Lord is one. You shall love the Lord your God with all your heart and with all your soul and with all your might. And these words that I command you today shall be on your heart."

These words should also be on your doorposts, wrists, walls, iPhone covers… and anywhere else you might see them. Why? Because the word of God has the power to change us. The word of God has the power to stir up love and obedience and sustain commitment year after year in every generation.

(ii) Isaiah 55:10-13

The second Old Testament passage is the stunning poetry of Isaiah 55:

> "For as the rain and the snow come down from heaven
> and do not return there but water the earth,
> making it bring forth and sprout,
> giving seed to the sower and bread to the eater,
> so shall my word be that goes out from my mouth;
> it shall not return to me empty,
> but it shall accomplish that which I purpose,
> and shall succeed in the thing for which I sent it.
>
> "For you shall go out in joy
> and be led forth in peace;
> the mountains and the hills before you
> shall break forth into singing,
> and all the trees of the field shall clap their hands.
> Instead of the thorn shall come up the cypress;
> instead of the brier shall come up the myrtle;
> and it shall make a name for the Lord,
> an everlasting sign that shall not be cut off."

The principle here is clear: God's word (which here is the message of the gospel, which has yet to be announced) will do exactly what God intends it to do. God's words always "succeed". But what's interesting here is the effect that these words produce. What does God's word do? It leads to people going out in joy and being led forth in peace. Not only does the gospel transform the world, it also changes the hearts of people like you and me.

Now while this is by no means all that Isaiah 55 has to teach us, Isaiah is clearly arguing that God works by getting his word under our skin.

Isaiah does not just tell us this is true, however. In his own ministry he spares no effort in getting the word of the Lord across to his peers. He uses poetry, prose, apocalyptic, symbolic action, warnings, laments. Why? Because he longs for people to be transformed by the power of the divine word. Even though he knows that for many his ministry will simply produce a hardening against God, he keeps going. As he communicates the word of God, he expects it to produce results at the deepest level in people's lives. Paul, in the New Testament, does no less.

(iii) 2 Timothy 3:14-17

> But as for you, continue in what you have learned and have firmly believed, knowing from whom you learned it and how from childhood you have been acquainted with the sacred writings, which are able to make you wise for salvation through faith in Christ Jesus. All Scripture is breathed out by God and profitable for teaching, for reproof, for correction, and for training in righteousness, that the man of God may be complete, equipped for every good work.

Though this is a familiar passage, I think we sometimes get the nuance of what Paul is saying slightly wrong. He is not speaking primarily about the 'usefulness' of the Scriptures. Paul is not saying that if we have to do some teaching or correcting or training, then the Bible is an extremely valuable resource. Rather, he is pointing out the way in which God works.

How does God make us "wise for salvation"? Through the Scriptures. How does God act—when he teaches, reproves, corrects and trains us? God equips us to live for him by shaping us through his word.

So how, then, should we teach? When Paul urges Timothy two verses later to "preach the word", he is urging him to uncage the lion, to let God speak through the Scriptures. And so when Paul underlines the importance of rebuking and exhorting and teaching, he is telling Timothy to allow the text to shape his message. When Timothy, or any of us, unleashes the illocutionary power of the Scriptures, the lion is let loose. Or, to use another scriptural metaphor, the sword of the word can do its work.

(iv) Hebrews 4:9-13

> So then, there remains a Sabbath rest for the people of God, for whoever has entered God's rest has also rested from his works as God did from his.
>
> Let us therefore strive to enter that rest, so that no-one may fall by the same sort of disobedience. For the word of God is living and active, sharper than any two-edged sword, piercing to the division of soul and of spirit, of joints and of marrow, and discerning the thoughts and intentions of the heart. And no creature is hidden from his sight, but all are naked and exposed to the eyes of him to whom we must give account.

There is some discussion about the nature of the 'rest' that God holds out to us in Jesus, but whether we take that to mean rest which starts now and goes on forever in Jesus, or simply the future rest which we look forward to in the new creation, it's clear that the way in which we enter that rest has something to do with "the word of God".

If our hearts are going to change and we are going to persevere and enter this rest, then we need God himself to show us our hearts and to change them with the skill of a surgeon. God uses the Bible to expose our thoughts and intentions. In other words, here again we see that our preaching will only change hearts if the Bible itself controls and defines the message we preach.

Passage by passage

Because the Bible is written in 'books', by far the best way to make sure that the message of the sermon matches the message of the passage is to work through books, passage by passage. (And, like John Calvin, you'll know exactly where to pick up where you left off!) As we'll explore in more depth in chapters 4 and 8, sermon series through books of the Bible need to move quickly enough to capture the flow of the book but slowly enough to allow people to get their heads around the details. This is usually called 'expository preaching' or 'systematic exposition'.

What does this actually look like? For Phil and me, it generally takes the shape of series of sermons that last, on average, about a school term (i.e. around 12 weeks). We move through whole books 'unit by unit', in a way that seeks to do justice both to the big idea of the individual unit (more on that in chapter 4) and to the flow and big idea of the book.

Preaching like this is hard work. And, in one sense, it doesn't get any easier the longer you're at it. That's why all of us need to develop a culture of lifelong learning. If we are going to take teaching the Bible seriously, then we will need to work at it constantly, developing our ability to understand, and teach, and apply, the Scriptures. Uncaging the lion involves rather a lot of hard work.

This approach ensures that your preaching will be both predictable and unpredictable. It will be predictable in the same way that the Bible is predictable. At the core of our preaching will be the same message—what God has already done for us in the Lord Jesus Christ. People can count on us, week after week, for the same thing: the Bible carefully, thoughtfully, engagingly explained.

I once had a conversation with a lady in our church who wasn't exactly a big fan of the Bible. "The problem with your sermons", she said, "is that they're all the same!" As I had just preached through Ephesians, Genesis and Mark's Gospel, I was a little puzzled. Then, in a rare moment of clarity, I answered, "Thank you very much!"

There is a sense in which every sermon we give should have the same message at its heart. We really do have only one thing to say. Of course, we should deliver that message in a myriad of ways. No two sermons should look the same or sound the same, but to careful listeners our sermons should always sound the same gospel note. They should be utterly predictable.

And yet, at the same time, our sermons should be deliciously unpredictable. Why? Because we have such fantastic source material, inspired by God himself, to change people's hearts.

Conclusion: The advantages of heart-changing, expository preaching

What are the advantages of teaching the Bible in this way?

Expository preaching:

1. does justice to the biblical material which makes it clear that God works through his word to change people's lives—as it 'uncages the lion' and allows God's word to speak.

2. acknowledges that it is God alone, through the Spirit, who works in people's lives, and that it is not our job to change people through clever or inspiring communication.

3. minimizes the danger of manipulating people, because the text itself controls what we say and how we say it. The Bible leaves little room for us to return repeatedly to our current bugbears and hobbyhorses.

4. minimizes the danger of abusing power, because a sermon driven by the text creates an instant safeguard against using the Bible to bludgeon (or caress) people into doing or thinking what we want them to do or think.

5. removes the need to rely on our personality. While we all feel the weight, at times, of having little 'inspiration', energy or creativity, if our focus is on allowing the immense richness of Scripture to speak in all its colour and variety, the pressure is well and truly off.

6. encourages humility in those teaching. While it can be a temptation to think that we are somehow special because we are standing at the front doing most of the talking (and, on a good day, receiving the encouragement), getting it straight that the key to preaching to the heart is simply uncovering the power and freshness of God's words helps to keep us in our place.

7. helps us to avoid simple pragmatism. If our focus is on working consistently to enable people to encounter the God who speaks through the text, we will not feel under pressure to address every single issue and topic as it comes up in the life of the church. Conversely, working through the Bible week by week will force us to cover subjects that we wouldn't choose to address in a million years. In other words, expository preaching is the simplest, longest-lasting antidote we have to pragmatism.

8. drives us to preaching the gospel. As we'll see in more detail in chapter 5, expository preaching is also uniquely valuable in that it persistently drives us to the Lord Jesus Christ (wherever we are in the Bible) and so 'forces' us to preach the gospel—that is, to spell out what God has already done for us in the death and resurrection of his Son, and then to move from that grace to what God asks and enables us to do. When we preach the gospel we are not simply telling people how to be good or leaving them to wallow in the overwhelming sense that they are irredeemably bad.

Only the gospel can change our hearts and minds. May we make it the great work of our lives to unleash the power of the gospel from all the Scriptures, and to say with Paul:

> I am not ashamed of the gospel, for it is the power of God for salvation to everyone who believes, to the Jew first and also to the Greek. For in it the righteousness of God is revealed from faith for faith, as it is written, "The righteous shall live by faith". (Rom 1:16-17)

But if people are going to hear the gospel, this "power of God for salvation", we need to explain it clearly and in an engaging way.

3

Deadly, dull and boring

So here are the true confessions you most want to hear from the guy who's writing the chapter on being clear and not being dull in this preaching book you just bought:

1. My battle with dullness hasn't been won, but I'm making steady progress.
2. I'm not a gifted natural communicator.
3. I'm uniquely qualified to write a chapter entitled 'Deadly, dull and boring'.

Let me explain. My early preaching disasters all followed the same deadly pattern. I'd write a well-crafted essay (much like the papers I'd write at theological college through the week), my wife, Louise, would read it and give the okay, and on Sunday morning I'd let it loose on the crowd.

But, time after time, it was the same train wreck. Parishioners would shake my hand at the door with a thin smile and a kind word, but the unvarnished truth always came out in the car trip home. I already knew what Louise was going to say. (I saw her slump sideways during the fifth sub-point.) "It looked great when I read through it yesterday—but today it was just so… boring." And I knew she was right.

"It's not you, it's me"

It's easy to blame the listener. Maybe it's the seven-minute attention span of 'the *Sesame Street* generation'. Or of those multi-tasking time-slicing you-phone i-tubers. Someone said to me just last week, "People these days just can't follow an intelligent argument". And, of course, there's some truth in that. Our culture has changed. Attention spans are shorter. We multi-task. We skim. We click, we like, we share, we move on to something else.

Jesus warns us to be careful how we listen, to avoid the fate of the ever hearing but never listening Israel (Matt 13:10-15). Sadly, some people just won't pay attention to God's word. And that's their problem.

But that wasn't the problem with my early sermons. I knew how hard it was to be a listener myself, and I knew how much more fun it was to count the bricks in the front wall of the church than to listen to a dull preacher. So I was convinced that it was my job to help my church family listen well… by working harder at keeping them awake. No more excuses. So one Sunday afternoon, I decided to make it my business to learn how to communicate.

I know some of you will think you've spotted the problem

already. Preaching from a written script, you'll say, is guaranteed to be dull. There's no connection with the congregation, there's no spontaneity. How can you expect the Spirit to move your listeners when you're preaching from a prepared text?

Let me share our little secret. Both Gary and I preach fully scripted. We're convinced that planning and preparing what you're going to say is not the problem—in fact, if you do it right, it's more often a solution.

We're not claiming this is the only way to preach—there are other models that work just fine. And I know it gets bad press. (If you're ready to dump this book right now, maybe you'll enjoy *Preaching without Notes* by Joseph M Webb, or the earlier work of John Broadus in his *Treatise on the Preparation and Delivery of Sermons*.[1])

Our point is this: if you master the art of *natural scripting*—writing exactly the words you'd naturally speak, exactly the way you'd naturally say them—then you can eliminate the downsides of scripted public speaking.

The first thing you need to realize is that natural scripting is completely different from writing an essay or a term paper. *That* was my problem. I didn't know the difference. But I soon learned, and most of what I learned will apply equally well to all sermon preparation—whether you're scripting your sermons or not.

Okay. Where did I start? My first step was to call my friend David Ritchie. Dave was a couple of years ahead of me at Sydney's Moore Theological College and an excellent natural communicator.

"Help!" I said. "I'm killing people. What am I doing wrong?"

Dave looked over my notes and saw the problem straight

---

1   Available as an ebook at www.openlibrary.org.

away. "You've got way too many ideas; too much content and too little repetition", he said. "I always repeat the first sentence of a new idea three times, to make sure people stay with me."

My next sermon was already in draft form, so I looked it over with new eyes. The process was painful. Ideas. Deleted. Topic sentences. Repeated. And repeated again. ("Not slavishly", said Dave. "Vary the words each time, but make sure you don't add any *new information*.")

More help came from Clifford Warne, veteran host of Australian Christian Television spots for kids, and master storyteller. When I asked him for tips, the answer came in the gift of the book *Say What You Mean* by Rudolf Flesch.[2] Oddly, it's a book about writing *business letters* in natural spoken style. But it was the breakthrough I was looking for. It's okay to use contractions like 'can't' and 'don't' and 'won't'. And it's okay to start sentences with conjunctions like 'and' and 'but', too. Even partial sentences are okay. Go on a 'which hunt', writes Flesch, and get rid of the 'thats' while you're at it. Simplify sentences. It was all about making communication clear, simple and direct. Between reading this book and taking Dave Ritchie's advice, my preaching changed overnight. (And my business letters did, too!)

So did it help? It still brings a tear to my eye as I remember the old guy who gripped my hand on the way out of church the next Sunday. "Young fella", he said warmly, "this morning *I was with you every step of the way*. Well done."

Louise was smiling too.

There was plenty more to learn, but I was thrilled to be connecting. I made it my business to figure out what works and what doesn't, to listen, think and measure. I work hard at

---

2   HarperCollins, New York, 1972. I recommend this, or any of Flesch's excellent books on clear communication and writing.

understanding the biblical text, and then I work just as hard at communicating it in a way that's clear and engaging and keeps people awake.

Scripting your sermon doesn't guarantee any of those things. But at least it enables you to plan, analyse and control what you intend to say and how you intend to say it. It helps you think through in advance how you'll pace the flow of ideas, and writing it down commits you to expressing yourself in a way that's down-to-earth and accessible. It also ensures you don't talk for too long. And that could save a life.

The new black

Perhaps the biggest benefit of all in scripting your sermon is that it can help you make things crystal clear. Clarity is 'the new black'. Just ask anyone with an iPad or an iPhone.[3] Apple designer Jony Ive explains it this way to *L'Uomo Vogue* magazine:

> The way we approach design is by trying to achieve the most with the very least. We are absolutely consumed by trying to develop a solution that is very simple because as physical beings we understand clarity, we're comfortable with clarity.[4]

Gary has been urging you to preach from the heart, and to the heart. I'm right there with him. But my brief is to push you to use your head—not to be more academically impressive, but to be clearer. At the end of his letter to the Colossians, Paul asks his friends to pray that God will equip him to preach.

---

3   It's also 'the new white'—depending on your choice of colour.
4   J Dalrymple, 'Jonathan Ive gives some insight into his designs', *The Loop*, 11 June 2009 (viewed 11 January 2013): www.loopinsight.com/2009/06/11/jonathan-ive-gives-some-insight-into-his-designs/

Look at his words:

> At the same time, pray also for us, that God may open
> to us a door for the word, to declare the mystery of
> Christ, on account of which I am in prison—*that I may
> make it clear, which is how I ought to speak.* (Col 4:3-4)

Paul's goal is *clarity*. Paul asks the Colossians to pray that through
his plain words, the previously hidden mystery of Christ would
be plain and obvious to all. He's not trying to be more eloquent;
he's not longing to be wittier or more entertaining. All he
wants is to be clear. (Though maybe Eutychus would suggest
Paul should also ask for prayer to know when to stop!)

He says the same thing to the Corinthians:

> And I, when I came to you, brothers, *did not come
> proclaiming to you the testimony of God with lofty speech
> or wisdom*. For I decided to know nothing among you
> except Jesus Christ and him crucified. (1 Cor 2:1-2)

> But we have renounced disgraceful, underhanded ways.
> We refuse to practice cunning or to tamper with God's
> word, but by *the open statement of the truth* we would
> commend ourselves to everyone's conscience in the
> sight of God. (2 Cor 4:2)

JC Ryle (1816-1900), the 19th-century Bishop of Liverpool,
was a smart guy. Schooled at Eton, he took first-class honours
at Oxford and was invited to join the faculty. But his goal was
ministry. When Ryle realized that he had affected a certain
'eloquent' style as a curate in Hampshire, however, he went
about trying to crucify this pretension. What he had thought
impressive was in fact completely counterproductive to gospel
preaching:

In fact, to use very long words, to seem very learned, to make people go away after a sermon, saying, "How fine! how clever! how grand!" all this is very easy work. But to write what will strike and stick, to speak or to write that which at once pleases and is understood, and becomes assimilated with a hearer's mind and a thing never forgotten—that, we may depend upon it, is a very difficult thing and a very rare attainment.[5]

Ryle found a mentor of sorts in George Whitefield (1714-70), whose sermons he studied. Ryle wrote:

Whitefield's preaching was *singularly lucid and simple...* His style was easy, plain, and conversational. He seemed to abhor long and involved sentences. He always saw his mark, and went direct at it... The consequence was, that his hearers always understood him. He never shot above their heads. Never did man seem to enter so thoroughly into the wisdom of Archbishop Usher's saying, "To make easy things seem hard is easy, but to make hard things easy is the office of a great preacher".[6]

Clarity. Being comprehensible without being condescending. Being simple without being simplistic. As Einstein put it, "Everything should be made as simple as possible, but no simpler".

I want to challenge you to work harder at preaching more clearly. I want to push you to prepare in a way that combines your heartfelt passion with hardheaded clarity, in a package

5   JC Ryle, 'Simplicity in Preaching', *The Briefing,* vol. 296, May 2003 (first published 1882), p. 16.
6   JC Ryle, *A Sketch of the Life and Labors of George Whitefield,* Waymark Books, Michigan, 2012, p. 52.

that's well planned, conversational and clear... and not too long. Are you ready for the challenge?

Top ten tips for being clearer

Paul asked the Colossians to pray that he'd preach with clarity, because he knew that it's hard to do so. As preachers, we should be praying that Colossians 4 prayer regularly and asking others to pray it for us. And then, like Jony Ive, we should be absolutely consumed by trying to design *sermons* that are simple without being simplistic, that are understandable and clear. We should try very hard to avoid *unnecessary complexity*.

Clarity comes from what you leave out. Clarity comes from focus. Usually, complexity comes from 'over-inclusion'. Over the years, I've developed a toolkit that I've passed on to a generation of students in my preaching classes. For those of you Letterman fans who were hoping you'd get at least one top-ten list of tips out of a book on preaching, here you are.

1. The more you say, the less people will remember

It's a fact of life. Why do most preachers want to talk longer than most people want to listen? The quote on my desk calendar tells me, "Biscuits and sermons are improved by shortening". In his song 'Long Sermon', country singer Brad Paisley bemoans the way long sermons on a pretty Sunday are a test of faith. Ecclesiastes 6:11 agrees: "The more the words, the less the meaning, and how does that profit anyone?" (NIV).

I know what he was saying was important, but if Paul hadn't talked on and on, Eutychus would have been spared lots of bruises. Say less. Please. Stop before someone dies.

So for how long should you preach? The answer for me is around 23 minutes. The answer for Gary is anywhere between

21 and 30 minutes, with an average around 25. The answer for Tim Keller is as long as he likes. The answer for all of us? Plan to stop a minute or two before people start wishing you would. (And stop thinking you're Tim Keller.)

2. Make the 'big idea' shape everything you say[7]

Here's the best way to trim an overgrown sermon. Apparently, a presidential speechwriter was once asked how he wrote such great speeches. "It's easy", he said. "First, I write a speech—then I take out all the bits that ain't great."

That's one of the best reasons to preach from a full script—you get to edit before you speak. You get to choose what you're going to say and what you're not. You get to take out all the bits that ain't going to be great.

And how do you decide what to take out and what to keep? Simple. Haddon Robinson says every sermon should grow from a *big idea* that you discover through hours of exegesis. You capture your big idea in a *single sentence summary* that states the essence of a passage and its application.[8] Robinson is right, and I know plenty of preachers who agree with him. The problem is, even after they've done the legwork and found the big idea, they usually don't stick to it. If you're anything like me, you'll find that other ideas scream for your attention like Siren-rocks; if you let them divert you, it won't be long until your once-clear big idea is sunk at the expense of every lesser idea that came to mind. These other ideas might even be noble ideas. And true. But leave them for another day and keep heading for your target.

---

7   What's the big idea? Chapter 4 will tell you everything you ever wanted to know about the 'big idea' and more.

8   HW Robinson, *Biblical Preaching: The development and delivery of expository messages,* 2nd edn, Baker, Grand Rapids, 2001.

Here's the tip. Once you've got the big idea, don't let go. Build your structure around it, then weigh every word and sentence to make sure it's pushing in the right direction. Don't be distracted by sidetracks when you're preparing, and your listeners won't be distracted while you're preaching. And, whatever you do, don't fall in love with your first draft—make every word and paragraph earn its place.

3. Choose the shortest, most ordinary words you can

It took me a while to realize that even the sharpest thinkers prefer simple, clear communication. And clear communication uses the simplest and clearest words you can find. This is one of the differences between written and spoken communication; we tend to use shorter words when we speak. Some words— like 'utilize'—are nothing but fancy, padded versions of a simpler, shorter word—like 'use'. When there's a choice, always use the shorter, simpler word.

Randall Munro, author of the popular webcomic *xkcd*, set himself the challenge of drawing NASA's Saturn V rocket and explaining it with vocabulary drawn only from the 1000 most common English words.[9] The "part that falls off first" and the "part that falls off second" are clearly marked, and there's not a 'capsule' or a 'cargo bay' in sight. Remarkably, it all makes immediate sense—to anyone. The more complex your subject, the more helpful it is to describe it in ordinary words.

I'm not just talking about not using jargon. I'm talking about syllables and the rhythms of natural conversation. I'm talking about using words that are easy to get your mouth around. I'm talking about using the words that you'd use in the kitchen or on the bus. I'm talking about choosing the clearest,

9   R Munro, 'Up Goer Five', *xkcd,* viewed 19 December 2012: www.xkcd.com/1133/

least stilted words you can. Listen to yourself sometime. And then eschew utilizing cumbersome terminology when a less pretentious vocabulary would adequately suffice.

4. Use shorter sentences

We package ideas in sentences. Listeners can't process an idea until they catch the sense of the sentence. So keep sentences short. According to the *Reader's Digest* style guide, the ideal average sentence length for a typical *Digest* reader (enriched word power and all) is between 17 and 20 words. That's surprisingly short—and it works quite well for sermons too. Take a moment to check the average sentence length in your last sermon. And find the 'readability score' of your sermon, too.[10] Aim for a score of 70 to 80 on the Flesch-Kincaid Reading Ease scale (yes, there's Rudolf Flesch again!), or 6.0 to 7.0 on the Flesch-Kincaid Grade Level calculator (this paragraph, for example, scores 73.5 and 5.7, respectively). The higher the score on the reading ease scale, the easier the text is to read. The highest possible score is around 120 (the *Harvard Law Review* has a score of around 30).

Don't be fooled. This isn't about 'dumbing down' your content. It's about communicating complex content clearly. (But keep in mind that alliteration is no longer considered tasteful.) More importantly, it's about sounding like a normal, conversational *you*. Gary's natural style is to use slightly longer sentences than I do. When he preaches, he sounds like Gary. I sound like me. Figure out what size sentences sound most like you—although if it comes out at over 127 words, it's time to revise your personality. Trust me. Between 17 and 20 is just fine.

---

10 You can paste your text and check your readability score at www.readability-score.com.

5. Forget everything your English teacher taught you

"Remember", said Bishop JC Ryle, "that English for speaking and English for reading are two different languages; and that sermons which preach well, always read ill".[11]

It's true. Which means if you're scripting a sermon you should expect it to read badly. It should break almost all the norms of good written expression and follow the rules of informal speech instead.

Listen to yourself in a normal conversation sometime and you'll realize that the order, sequence and styling of your words break all the rules of formal writing. The formal rules of essay writing taught by old-school English teachers are the conventions and rules that are most likely to make a scripted sermon sound artificial and stilted.

Remember, your goal is to script your sermon in exactly the way *you* usually speak. So try these naughty tricks:

- Boldly start sentences with 'And' or 'But'. Or even 'Or'. It's usually considered bad form for writing, but it's great for speaking. Listen to yourself sometime… we almost always do it when we're chatting.
- Contract. Use contracted forms such as 'can't', 'don't', 'won't', 'aren't'… along with all the other abbreviations we naturally use in daily speech. The only exception I can think of is that sometimes you might choose to use a fully formed 'not' for impact and emphasis. Gleefully write the contractions into your text in exactly the way you'd talk to a friend, all the while ignoring the scolding of your old English teacher in your head. And, if you compose onscreen, turn off the spell and grammar

11   Ryle, *Sketch*, p. 50.

checks if those wrist-slapping underlines distract you from writing the real you. (Although I tend to read the squiggly lines now as a sign that I'm on the right track!)

- Avoid complex, multi-clause sentence structures. We usually speak in simple, direct sentences. Sometimes not sentences at all! Can you learn to write like that? That's why Rudolf Flesch was so keen to get rid of 'thats' and 'whiches'—they always introduce subordinate clauses, which are harder for listeners to process.

6. Am I repeating myself?

In natural spoken communication, we repeat ourselves often. It's vital. If you're reading, you'll create your own repetitions by re-reading a difficult section until you're ready to move forward. (Why not go back and read that last sentence again?) When you're preaching, listeners don't have the same luxury, and it's up to you to anticipate where they'll need help. As I said earlier, Dave Ritchie taught me that as you're introducing a new idea, it's incredibly helpful to restate the first sentence three times, rephrasing it each time but adding no new information. Effectively, the first statement signals that you've changed tack, the second helps the listener to start processing the new idea, and the third time begins the next part of the journey.

Repetition is also the way you'll emphasize key points, and it's a great tool for breaking up those long, multi-clause sentences. For instance, "It's awful to sit through a long, dull, repetitive sermon" has loads more punch when you're speaking if you replace it with, "*It's awful* to sit through a *long* sermon… *It's awful* to sit through a *dull* sermon. It's *awful, really awful,* to sit through a *repetitive* sermon."

Why does repetition help? Because, more than anything else, repetition regulates the information flow. Too much information, flowing too quickly, makes people feel like they're drinking from a fire hose. Avoid giving too much information and learn the difference between the pace of your speech (in 'words per minute') and the pace of information (in 'ideas per minute'). Getting a feel for the right balance between repetition and forward movement is the key here. Too many ideas per minute, and people will feel it's too complex—slow it down by adding some strategic repetition and explanation. Slow down the idea stream too much, though, and you'll sound condescending—you'll be 'labouring the point'. It's difficult to find the right balance, but the first step is to be aware that you need to.

Words per minute versus ideas per minute

What do I mean? Below, you'll see 223 words from a sermon I preached on Saul's conversion in Acts 9. At my usual speech rate of around 150 words per minute, these paragraphs would take around a minute and a half to deliver. In those 223 words you'll find a grand total of two ideas. See if you can spot them…

> I want you to think for a minute about the person in your life who's the least person likely who you know to ever become a Christian. The person who's the most hostile to the Christian faith. Most disparaging. The one who laughs loudest at the idea of God. At the name of the Lord Jesus. And now I want you to double it. Double… the derision. Double… the disdain. Double… the barbed remarks and the cynicism. Until you've got the worst-case scenario. And then… you've got Saul. Who we first met at the very start of Acts chapter 8.
>
> If you've been watching the tennis on TV lately you'll be noticing the ball boys and the ball girls. Pumped up and ready at each end of the court to dash after the

ball. They're the kids who'd love to one day be out there on centre court. They're looking on in admiration, helping however they can in the hope one day they'll make the big time. Saul, when we last met him, was like that. Except it wasn't tennis they were playing… but stoning. And Saul was the little guy on the sidelines looking after their coats. Helping. However he could. While they stoned Stephen to death.

After all that repetition (which is annoying to read on the page, I know), I hope you picked up the first idea: "Saul is twice as unlikely as anyone you know to become a Christian."

The second idea flows straight on from the first: "When we first met Saul in the book of Acts, he was helping to stone Stephen."

I could have delivered those two ideas in just 29 words, and then used my spare 194 words to squeeze in 13 more ideas. If you'd been there listening, you would have been glad I didn't. Repetitions like "most hostile", "most disparaging" and "laughs loudest" are all making exactly the same point but, like the tennis illustration, they're slowing the flow of ideas to the point where a listener can easily absorb them.

7. Translate narratives into the present tense

This tip is great. It works. I love it. I've regularly had people tell me I've brought a biblical narrative to life… and I give a wry smile, knowing that all I've done is translate the text into present tense. It looks odd when you put it on paper, but have you ever noticed how often jokes are told in the present tense? ("Did you hear the one about the Irishman and the Australian who *walk* into a pulpit…?") The same often applies to TV news reports, especially in headlines and video voiceovers. ("Riots *erupt* on city streets today as ice cream supplies *run* low.")

Odd as it seems, translating narrative into the present tense makes a story seem real and immediate—it's just like being there. Retell a biblical narrative with present tense verbs, and something refreshing happens. The same applies to illustrations. You can take your listeners back in time and put them right inside the action just by adjusting the tenses… they *look*, he *whispers*, he *says*. It's alive! Keeping narratives in the past tense coats everything with dust.

As a side note, this tool works for retelling content from the epistles as well. Put yourself right beside Paul as he writes, and relay what he's saying in the present tense. (You probably do this already, because you're convinced the Bible is a living book. For example, I would naturally say, "The apostle Paul *says*, 'The life I now live in the body, I live by faith in the Son of God.'" That's because he didn't '*said*' it. He still '*says*' it.)

8. The six-million-dollar secret of illustrating

Illustrations are great for explaining complex ideas and touching emotions and applying your main point. But they're also a great way to keep your listeners fresh by giving them a break. If you've ever struggled to find just the right illustration, this tip is solid gold.

Here it is: Don't sweat over illustrating the complicated stuff—just illustrate the obvious!

When the pressure is off, illustrating becomes incredibly easy. The simple images and ideas in your passage will trigger all the stories and associations you need; you'll be swamped with possibilities, and you can use them when you need them. As an exercise in my preaching class, I give students two minutes to think of a real-life story to illustrate Amos 8:2:

"What do you see, Amos?" [the Lord] asked.

"A basket of ripe fruit", I answered.

Then the Lord said to me, "The time is ripe for my people Israel; I will spare them no longer". (NIV)

Try it yourself. Ripe fruit. In fact, Israel is overripe. Remember the banana you left in your school bag for a few months? Or that orange at the bottom of the fruit bowl growing a coat of blue-green mould? The peaches on the tree at the bottom of the garden, ready to be plucked? Every student in the class could think of a story like that in moments. Start illustrating the obvious and you'll find so many ideas for rest-stop illustrations that you'll find it easy to keep your listeners bright and fresh. The secret? Illustrate the obvious, and the complex ideas will take care of themselves, because your listeners will be fresh and focused enough to stay with you. It's kind of like taking breaks with kids on a car trip. Sometimes it's smart to stop where there's a restroom whether they need it or not—the kids may not thank you, but on the next stage of the journey they'll be glad you did.

9. People love to hear about people

Take a look at the front page of a newspaper sometime. Are interest rates rising? Then you're almost sure to see a photograph of an affected family. Graphs and statistics can come later. The journalist's rule is this: if there are no people, there's no story. So populate your preaching with real people. Use people-based illustrations and people-based application. Where you can, talk about real people and real situations, instead of just talking about abstract ideas. Typically, I'll scour the newspaper, internet news sources and TV for fresh material. Incredibly, there always seems to be something useful. Of course, if the story involves a member of your congregation then you'll need to ask permission first.[12]

10. Work towards your key text

Here's my final top-ten tip. But it's probably the best. In this book we're assuming a commitment to expository preaching, which means that week by week you'll be bringing your congregation face to face with the text of Scripture.

That's going to involve highlighting and explaining key texts from the passage as you speak. Here's the tip. When you're quoting a verse, help out the listener by setting it up *before* you read it, rather than after.

In other words, lead your listeners *towards* the text. Instead of quoting it then explaining it, do the reverse. Explain and then show. Prepare them for the logic of what they're about to see for themselves in Scripture by raising the question the text is about to answer, or by building the logic of the argument that the text itself is about to resolve, or by explaining anything complex that they'll need to understand to make sense of it. Then, let the words of Scripture close the deal.

When you work in the other direction, reading the verse then unpacking it, you're asking your listeners to hold the words of Scripture in their heads while you go on to explain them. It's tough work for the listener, and disengaging. Try it the other way around.

---

12   In fact, even if it's about one of your kids make sure you ask permission first! Being a pastor's kid carries enough baggage without growing up in church where everyone can recite the 'cute stories' of your childhood.

SO THERE THEY ARE—my ten top tips for preaching more clearly. My guess is that at least eight out of these ten tips are familiar to you already. In fact, I've noticed that most natural communicators—whether scripted or not—tend to do most of these things by instinct. But even if you think it's obvious, we need to keep in mind the even more obvious fact that communication hasn't happened until the message has been received at the other end. I've sat through sermons where it feels like the preacher is talking on the phone before he's dialled the number; there's nobody on the other end of the line. I've *heard* sermons like that? To be honest, I've *preached* sermons like that! And as Louise still sometimes reminds me at the door, it's usually because I've forgotten something obvious. You'll find these tips in a checklist format at the end of this book (appendix 2). My suggestion is that you run through the list quickly before you start your sermon preparation each week, and then again as you finalize what you're going to say. Sanctifying as it is to be reminded you're far from perfect by pseudo-polite parishioners at the door (and an honest wife on the car ride home), it's far nicer to see a smile and hear a "Well done, young fella, this morning I was with you every step of the way".

4

So what's the big idea?

It's not nice to throw sand

British Prime Minister Winston Churchill once said of a colleague, "He is one of those orators who, before he gets up, does not know what he is going to say; when he is speaking, does not know what he is saying; and when he sits down, doesn't know what he has said".[1]

I'm one of those orators too. Or I can be. With Sunday looming, I'm always tempted to start writing my sermon before I've worked out what my passage is really all about. But the truth is, I can't do anything useful until the big idea of my

[1] In JC Maxwell, *Everyone Communicates, Few Connect: What the most effective people do differently,* Thomas Nelson, Nashville, 2010, p. 157.

passage is crystal clear. Sure, I can start writing a sermon—and it's tempting to think I'm being productive. But with no idea of what I really need to be saying, it's actually not productive at all.

Maybe it's just me, but I find that understanding a text is never easy. On first reading, every part of the Bible I've ever tried to preach on seems totally opaque. Sure, God's word is sharper than a two-edged sword… but most days my brain is duller than a bowl of mush. For me it's always slow work. It's always hard work. I'm almost always ready to give up in despair. Almost every week, I'm tempted to start writing the sermon before I've really understood the passage, just so I'll have something to say on Sunday. Anything.

My advice? Resist the temptation. It's obvious. Your sermon will have no focus. That's guaranteed—because you haven't aimed it anywhere. It's going to be a case of 'ready, fire, aim' rather than 'ready, aim, fire' and, by the time you sit down at the end of your sermon, nobody will have a clue what you just said. Not even you.

In his book *Christ-Centered Preaching*, Bryan Chapell agrees:

> Without a clear purpose, listeners have no reason to listen… All good communication requires a theme. If the preacher doesn't provide it, listeners will instinctively try to find a unifying thought.[2]

In short, he says, it's easier for your listeners to catch a baseball than a handful of sand.

Take note that the theme he's talking about isn't arbitrary or artificial. It's the freshly-squeezed essence of the passage. The

2   B Chapell, *Christ-Centered Preaching: Redeeming the expository sermon,* Baker, Grand Rapids, 2005, p. 37.

meaning (or 'vibe') of the passage then becomes the message (or 'vibe') of the sermon, as we saw in chapter 2.[3]

Of course, squeezing the essence from a passage usually involves sweat and tears, and it's tempting to take shortcuts. We'll impose our own agenda on the text and use it as a springboard for our favourite hot topic. Or we'll grab the first idea in the text that comes to mind and force the logic to fit. Or we'll preach a whole string of ideas, without any effort to relate them to one another at all—a smorgasbord from which listeners can pick and choose as they like. A handful of sand. Or we'll just start writing… with no idea at all.

Stop. Don't do it. Before you do anything else, you need to uncover the elusive big unifying idea of the passage you're unpacking. But how?

There's a prior problem. First you have to decide the size and shape of the passage you'll be preaching. How do you do that? How many verses? A paragraph or two? A chapter? Maybe even more?

Each week, the answer will be different. Though it would be convenient for preachers if the universe worked the other way round, the underlying idea defines the size of your 'expository unit'—so you'll need to catch on to the idea before you can properly see the edges of the passage. The first reading of the text feels a bit like walking through a wheat field looking for a corn patch—you'll only know where the corn starts when you see corn. Sadly, the traditional fence lines are not much help. Stephen Langton sliced the Bible into chapters in the 12th century, and Robert Estienne added verse markers in 1551 on a horse ride from Paris to Lyons. Some think the horse would have done better.

---

3   Although when you're preaching from the Old Testament, the meaning of the passage *viewed through the lens of the gospel* becomes the message of the sermon.

This process sometimes takes me a few attempts. I'll survey a book and make rough cuts, then I'll refine the expository units as I do more detailed work on the text.

Uncovering the big idea

Okay. Let's assume you've defined your passage boundaries and are ready to start work. If you've had theological training, you'll know that skills in the original biblical languages can be a great help. There's often a precision of tenses and vocabulary that our English translations either overlook or can't quite capture. More significantly, some English translations tend to hide verbal repetitions in the original text for stylistic reasons—but in making the translation more readable, they obscure the original point.

But if you can't tell an *alpha* from an *aleph*, don't panic. We're about to look at some straightforward and practical ways to dig through the text of whatever Bible translation is sitting on your desk.

Come into my study on a Tuesday morning and have a seat. You'll need a Bible and some outmoded tools: paper and a pen.

My first step with every sermon is to write out my passage *by hand* on blank paper divided into two columns—the left-hand column takes up around two-thirds of the page. (Yes, I know I could copy and paste the text with my computer, or even retype it, much faster than I can write it by hand. But I don't, because old-fashioned handwriting activates a different set of brain pathways, slows me down, and helps me see and digest the text up close, one thought at a time.)

Translate the passage from the original language if you can do it quickly, but otherwise just copy word by word from a good English translation. Fill that wide left column until your hand hurts, and then write some more. As you write, arrange sentences and paragraphs visually according to the logic of the passage. If you've ever learned a programming language, follow the same rules. Here are some examples:

- indent anything following a *because* or *since* or *therefore* to show how it flows from the prior clause
- group *if* and *then* statements to highlight the connections
- show listed items in a sentence as a bulleted list, for example:
  - I pray this for you
  - and this for you…

- highlight repeated grammatical forms by aligning them.

As you go, make a note in the right-hand column about anything that strikes you as significant or puzzling. These bits are usually the most rewarding. Use your Bible software or an online reference like www.Biblestudytools.com to drill back to the original language at these points and make notes of any key findings, again in the right-hand column. As you progress, summarize each paragraph or movement of thought, again in the right-hand column, and keep revising the summary that's building up as you work.

Here's where it really gets messy. I'm a visual learner, so I highlight repeated words and ideas by circling or underlining them, usually with a coloured marker pen, then I scrawl bold linking lines between them across the text. This is the key: *noticing repeated words or phrases is the most common and most obvious way of finding the big idea of a passage.* Just as we use repetition for emphasis when we're preaching, if a writer wants us to notice something important they'll say it a number of times. *The big idea of a passage most often emerges when you spot the repetitions in the text and follow the chain of logic between them.*

I often think of this process as tunnelling sideways, mining for the seam that runs *along* the logic of the text. But at this point I also dig downwards, and track back cross-references and allusions in the text. If I'm working on a passage in the New Testament, I'll start by following any direct Old Testament references… then I'll read a few chapters around the text being quoted and look at the context. This is often fertile soil, as you'll notice later in the worked example of Acts 8 in chapter 8. In spite of what you might have heard, New Testament writers seldom quote without context—and they almost always have the big picture in mind.

If I'm preaching on an Old Testament passage, I'll look for back-references to foundational passages like the covenant promises to Abraham in Genesis 12, or the restoration promises of Deuteronomy 30:1-6. The themes and promises in these passages undergird Old Testament theology. And sometimes those background connections are more helpful

SO WHAT'S THE BIG IDEA?

than I expect them to be. It's just that I'm not sure yet, so all these thoughts, ideas and references go in the increasingly chaotic right-hand column of my page.

When I finish all the copying and scribbling, a couple of things happen. First, I stop for a cup of tea. I deserve it. Second, I look back over my visual map of the passage and retrace the logic. I try to summarize the flow of the passage by looking through the words and ideas I've highlighted. I try to fit them into a sentence that describes the grammatical shape of the passage: "Since x, then y, so you should not think z."

Best of all, after all that writing I've finally embedded the words and flow of the passage in my mush-bowl brain. Now it's with me while I'm walking or showering or going to sleep. It's with me while I'm digging through commentaries. It's with me while I think about the connection between the big idea in the passage, as it's *mediated by Jesus*, and my own life, and then the lives of the people in my church. When I've got that clear, I'm ready to start working on the sermon. When I haven't got that clear, I've got nothing to talk about!

One of the most frustrating things about teaching the Bible regularly is that we have to start from scratch every time. Every Monday (unless you are very organized) there's another blank sheet and the gnawing fear that in six days' time you will have nothing to say (or that what you do have won't be worth saying). I don't think that feeling ever goes away. But that's probably no bad thing. In fact, that's almost certainly the way God has set it up—because he knows that in our weakness, he is strong (2 Cor 12:9).

Application station

This is probably a good time to talk about application. When you're speaking on Sunday, that's what everyone's holding out for—especially the drowsy ones. I can almost hear them saying, "Let's just cut to the chase". So here are four practical tips for getting practical.

(i) Apply in the light of the gospel

First and foremost, keep in mind the point we've been making already. If you're preaching from the Old Testament, which was directed first and foremost to Israel, remember your audience: mainly Gentile, post-Jesus, predominantly Christian. Struggling Christians, confused Christians, self-righteous Christians. You hope that there will be non-Christian visitors every week too, and that they will catch hold of the gospel—*even when you're preaching from the Old Testament*. It's important to remember your audience, no matter what part of the Bible you're preaching from, and to make sure you never just assume *the gospel*, even if you're preaching from 'the gospels' or epistles.

Here's the problem. No matter where you're preaching from, it's easy to lose sight of the gospel of *what Jesus has done* and replace it with a whole lot of concrete and persuasive and guilt-inducing applications about *what we need to do*.

This kind of "therefore you should…" application is an obvious problem in the Old Testament and one that a number of good books about biblical theology address.[4] It's not so obvious when it comes to the gospels; more often than we sometimes notice, Jesus is aiming his words directly at an Israel at the tail end of their old covenant with God. It's pre-cross Israel and pre-Spirit Israel. Think the words of Jesus through carefully before

---

4   Graeme Goldsworthy's *Gospel and Kingdom* (Paternoster, Milton Keynes, 2012) is still my favourite because it's so startlingly clear. And brief! His later books, like *Preaching the Whole Bible as Christian Scripture,* are more nuanced—and longer. Bryan Chapell's *Christ-Centered Preaching* is helpful too.

you apply them directly to 21st-century Gentiles like us.[5]

Be careful in the epistles too. Paul commonly spells out the good news of the gospel in his opening chapters, drops in a massive 'therefore' (e.g. Rom 12:1), and then spends the following chapters explaining how to live for Jesus in response to God's grace in the gospel. If you forget to mention the reasons before the 'therefore', you're just dishing up a to-do list without anchoring it in the gospel. Gospel application always builds on the fact that Christians celebrate both the finished work of Christ for us and the Spirit's work in us in a way that Israel could only ever dream of.

Of course, that doesn't mean that we won't need to be corrected, or that we won't need to be continually repenting, or that we don't need constant reminders to 'be what we are'. It's a mistake to think you can ever hold back on application because you're talking to a bunch of 'nice people' in church. Paul had to remind the Ephesian Christians to stop lying and stealing. And, in my experience, every Sunday across my smiling congregations I'll be talking to at least two or three men on the brink of a catastrophic office romance, three or four guys struggling with same-sex attraction, and a hundred and fifty or so—all of them—drawn to internet pornography like flies to a honey pot. And that's just the men. And they're all smiling at me as if they've got it all together.

Messy? Yes. But the reality of sin reminds us that it's all the more important to keep looking through that gospel lens as we move to application instead of just making more rules.

---

5   Luke 11:13 is a prime example of this. When Jesus encourages his disciples to pray and knock and seek, knowing "how much more will the heavenly Father give the Holy Spirit to those who ask him", he's calling them to pray for the successful outcome of his mission. At this point, the long-promised Spirit has not yet come. If you're preaching that "If you pray more, God will give you *more* of the Spirit", you're really missing his point. The Spirit *came*... just as they prayed!

Because, as Paul says, Israel's rules could never change hearts (e.g. Gal 5:4-5).

(ii) Apply what the passage is *really* saying

There's another danger in application, and it's a subtle one. We saw it in the prologue, when John Chapman reminded Bill Hybels—and all of us—of the vital importance of preaching only what the passage is actually saying. It starts innocently enough. First it's just preaching right doctrine from the wrong text, blurring the distinction between your own 'good advice' and God's clear direction. The trouble is, what happens when it becomes the *wrong doctrine* from the wrong text? Or your own *bad* advice? Will anybody know the difference? In earlier times, preachers took more care with this. Eighteenth-century clergyman Charles Simeon said,

> My endeavour is to bring out of Scripture what is there, and not to thrust in what I think might be there. I have a great jealousy on this head; never to speak more or less than I believe to be the mind of the Spirit in the passage I am expounding.[6]

We should do the same—and the best way to be sure that we're bringing out of Scripture only what is there is to work hard on getting hold of the big, integrating idea of the passage before we do anything else.

(iii) Unflinching application

With these precautions in mind, it's worth remembering that every part of Scripture was originally written with a pastoral

6   In HCG Moule, *Charles Simeon,* IVP, Leicester, 1952, p. 77.

intention—it was meant to be applied. The original authors always intended their audience to think or do something differently as a result of hearing or reading their words.

When you've worked hard at discerning that pastoral intention, whatever you do, don't flinch at the point of application. Don't be timid. There's nothing duller than dishwater preaching. But always mix boldness with grace. It's important to say what you mean, without being *mean* in what you say. Or, as Paul puts it in Ephesians 4:15, "speaking the truth in love, we are to grow up in every way into him who is the head, into Christ".

Of course, sometimes there's an 'elephant in the room'—an issue so obvious, and so directly related to the passage, that it's embarrassing for everyone (a recent divorce, perhaps, when you're preaching on Malachi 2). It's almost never okay to identify a specific situation; and it's sometimes wise to contact affected people before a sermon to let them know what the passage is about. You'll sometimes struggle to find exactly the right words and tone, and you'll need to pray for sensitivity to recognize the times when people don't need to be rebuked because they're feeling badly enough already. In Bryan Chapell's words, "say exactly what you mean exactly as you'd say it to a loved one".[7] Gently.

Finally, don't hide behind 'we' when it comes to application, and take particular care to avoid the ever-popular string of rhetorical "*Do we…*" questions. Gary, who emphasizes that we should always flag the fact that as preachers we're including ourselves in every point of application, thinks I push this point a bit too hard. Agreed. But too many rhetorical 'we-questions' can tend to sound soppy rather than humble. (Though never when Gary does it!) Be direct. "If *you* are on the verge of an

---

7   Chapell, *Christ-Centered Preaching,* p. 223.

affair with that girl who understands you at the office, *don't do it!*" carries much more punch than the vague, "Do we sometimes struggle with sexual temptation?" It's important that, as the preacher, you acknowledge that you struggle with sin and are dependent on the gospel—though you should avoid using your congregation as your therapist! Look for balance and you'll find it somewhere between honesty and over-sharing, between authority as a preacher of God's word and helpful vulnerability as a fellow traveller.

(iv) Application last and first

When Jesus said that the last shall be first and the first last, he probably wasn't talking about sermon application. But it's a good thing to keep in mind. It's important that the application is the *last thing* you think about as you work on a passage, because if you start applying before you've caught the big idea, you'll be missing the point. Ultimately, though, when you finally have a clear grasp of the message of the passage, and you've worked out how it applies, your application is going to shape your sermon—because your *application* is where you're heading. It's going to be the point that you're driving towards, the reason you're standing to speak, and the lasting impact when you finally sit down. In other words, your applied big idea will be first and foremost in your mind as you start to write your sermon. In the words of Haddon Robinson, "Application starts in the introduction, not in the conclusion".[8] Here's the twist: the application comes at the end of your research, but it comes first as you design and build your sermon. If you take a look at the sample sermon in chapter 8, for example, the big idea of the passage (Acts 8) is that Samaritans and

8   Robinson, *Biblical Preaching,* p. 164.

foreigners are now included in Christ. My *applied* big idea was that people beyond our own comfortable boundaries should be welcomed and included in our church. It's *that idea* that shapes the opening and structure of the sermon.

Gary wrote the following to explain the process behind his sermon 'Life in a Changed World' on Acts 3:1-4:12:[9]

> As I was trying to work out the big idea of the passage, I realized how new—and strange—it was that the man was healed "in the name of Jesus". When I noticed that this same phrase is used in Acts 4:10-12 (which is clearly important), I was on my way. The fact that everything and everyone changes in this section led to the simple big idea: the coming of Jesus Christ changes everything and has the power to change us.

WHEN YOU HAVE the goal in mind of applying God's truth to people's lives, you can be confident. You can be confident that by the time you get up to speak you'll know exactly what you're going to say. You can be confident that you'll know what you're saying while you're saying it. You can be confident that when you sit down everyone, including you, will know exactly what you've said. And you can be confident that God will take it from there to transform hearts and lives.

9   See appendix 1 for the text of this sermon.

.

5

Why preaching the gospel is so hard
(especially from the Old Testament)

JUST ABOUT THE WORST THING that can happen when we finish preaching is that someone will walk out the door of the church buoyed by their own resolve to try harder. As we've seen in chapter 4, no matter what the passage is, it's essential that we never bury the gospel of *what Jesus has done* in an avalanche of great ideas about *what we need to do*. We want to preach *the gospel*—that is, we want to remind people of the grace that God has shown us in the Lord Jesus Christ; exhort people to take hold of that grace; and encourage them to go and live for and with Christ in the power of that grace. We want to encourage people, not crush them. We want people to be filled with joy, not loaded with guilt. Where we preach the gospel, people are encouraged and filled with grace and joy. The problem (which you will know very well if you've ever tried it) is that preaching the gospel is much more difficult than it looks. It's like hitting a straight drive on the golf course. We try to hit it straight, but the ball is always hooking into the rough of legalism or disappearing into the pond of powerless, feel-good licence (as John Bunyan might have said if he'd ever played golf).

This is a challenge when we preach from the New Testament. But it is even more difficult when we try to preach the gospel from the Old Testament, because it involves several more steps and we can start to veer off-course at any one of those. First we need to get our Old Testament hermeneutics right (that is, we need to read the Old Testament correctly), then we need to get our biblical theology right (we need to make sure we understand the passage properly in the context of the whole Bible). Finally, we need to preach the gospel (or take people to the work of Jesus) in a way that is true to the text but is not utterly predictable or, you guessed it, deadly boring.

But don't panic yet—plenty of help is at hand. First, we'll take a look at the hermeneutics of preaching Christ from the Old Testament; then we'll explore finding a route to the gospel through biblical theology.

Reading the Bible in stereo: The hermeneutics of preaching Christ

My extensive research (which has involved listening to myself, and occasionally other people, preach over the past 25 years) has shown that preaching dull sermons is much easier to do from the Old Testament than from the New. An experienced preacher (or even an inexperienced one) can happily set off for a wander through the text, secure in the knowledge that within minutes at least half of the listeners will be either catching up on lost sleep or counting the bricks… again. But if the snoring is getting on your nerves, the building committee already has an accurate brick count, and the people in your congregation need to hear the gospel, let's see what we can do.

The first problem is that, most of the time, we read the Bible in 'mono'. I was thoroughly depressed last week when Maddie, my PA, informed me that she wasn't even born when U2 released *The Joshua Tree*. If you're also too young to remember this momentous occasion in rock and roll history, you may be surprised to learn that there was something before stereo: it was called *mono*. In the world way back then, all the sound came through one speaker. I can still remember the thrill of hearing the richness of stereo sound as the speakers were plugged in for the first time to our National Panasonic Hi Fi (complete with plastic 'smoked glass' lid). *Different* sounds came from *each* speaker—it was so cool (we were easily impressed back then).

Why am I telling you this? The problem with many Old Testament sermons is that they're based on a 'mono' reading of the text. Either the sermon comes to us through the speaker of the past (what happened way back then has nothing to do with *us* and is therefore irrelevant), or the sermon makes it sound as though what happened way back then had nothing to do with *them* and was provided only as sermon fodder for *us* (and therefore lacks authenticity). Either way, these sermons sound flat and a bit tinny. The 'trick' is to read the Old Testament in *stereo*—with an understanding that it was written for us *and* for them. We need to read and experience *the whole Bible*. Only when we experience the richness of what God has done for his people throughout salvation history can we have this 'surround sound' experience God designed.

The hermeneutical mistake preachers make over and over again when it comes to preaching the Old Testament is that we tend to read it only one way—either we read it *forwards* (that is, as if it were a purely Jewish text) or we read it *backwards* (as if it were a purely Christian text). But if we are to preach Christ effectively, we need to understand the Old Testament as part of the Christian Scriptures and read it as carefully as we do the New Testament. The Old Testament, as Paul reminds us in 1 Corinthians 10:9-13, was written for them *and* for us:[1]

> We must not put Christ to the test, as some of them did and were destroyed by serpents, nor grumble, as some of them did and were destroyed by the Destroyer. Now these things happened *to them* as an example, but they were written down *for our instruction*, on whom the end of the ages has come. Therefore let anyone who thinks that he stands take heed lest he fall. No temptation has overtaken you that is not common to man. God is faithful, and he will not let you be tempted beyond your ability, but with the temptation he will also provide the way of escape, that you may be able to endure it.

Paul says that these things *happened to them* but were *written for us.* In that one simple sentence, I think we can find the hermeneutical key to preaching Christ effectively, helpfully, and in a way that makes people gasp. Here's how to preach the Old Testament in stereo.

---

1   The 'us' and 'them' vocabulary here simply makes a distinction between Christians and the Old Testament people of God.

It happened to them

This is basically reading the Bible *forwards*—with a sensitivity to the Old Testament as the record of God's dealings with a particular group of people in their particular historical circumstances. We need to start with the fact that the Bible was written *for them*. Whether the 'them' is Moses' generation, or those in Jeremiah's day staring the Exile in the face, or those apathetic second- and third-generation returnees who were the bane of Malachi's life, the Bible was in at least one sense written *for them*.

You can see this perspective elsewhere in the New Testament —in Romans 9:3-5, for example, at the start of Paul's discussion of the fact that relatively few Jews have become Christians:

> For I could wish that I myself were accursed and cut off from Christ for the sake of my brothers, my kinsmen according to the flesh. They are Israelites, and to them belong the adoption, the glory, the covenants, the giving of the law, the worship, and the promises. To them belong the patriarchs, and from their race, according to the flesh, is the Christ, who is God over all, blessed forever.

Because we are not Jews, the Old Testament is not about us. It happened to them.

As we think about what it means for us to read the Old Testament through New Testament eyes and distinguish between 'us' and 'them', it's helpful to keep the following in mind.[2] We need to keep a firm grip on the fact that we're *the Gentiles* that Paul keeps talking about—the ones with whom

---

2   Phil, who worked for a few years in a context with a tradition of Old Testament legalism, has thought through many of these issues.

the Old Testament Jews wanted very little to do. Even the verses above from Romans 9 point that out. The covenants and the law *and the promises* all belonged to *Israel*, and not to the Gentiles. Though now, according to Ephesians 2, if you're a *Gentile by birth* who has faith in Jesus then you can enjoy the benefits of the *promise* without the burden of the law (which was fulfilled by Jesus before we were even invited to the party).

In short, it's helpful to remember that we're late arrivals who are only here because Jesus invited us. As Gentiles, we were *never* under the law—and the meeting of the council of Jerusalem in Acts 15 resolved that we never should be. So if you're wondering whether it's okay to eat the shrimp cocktail or the bacon and egg sandwich, the answer is *yes* for two reasons. First, you're a Gentile. The Old Testament law excluded you from its regulations. Second, Christ has now fulfilled Israel's law anyhow. We need to read the Old Testament as *late arrivals* or as *adopted children* looking back at the family tree of the beloved family we've been joined to. As newcomer Gentile Christians we have plenty to learn about the God who always planned to include us, and about the privileges and blessings of the family we've been joined to and the nature of godly living as well. And we have all the privileges of having joined the family in this new age of the Spirit without ever having had to live under the law.

As Paul says, those of us who are Gentiles need to be careful that we don't end up under the law all over again. But if we ignore the Old Testament completely just because we're Gentile readers (as I suspect most of us are), we'll miss a significant part of the message of the gospel, the good news which God begins to reveal in Genesis. Because although it happened to them, it has huge significance for us.

It was written for us

Paul insists that while all this happened to *them,* it was very definitely written for *us,* on whom the end of the ages has come. Christians don't often appreciate that this truth works at two levels.

For Christians

Paul clearly believes that the Old Testament is ultimately written for us *as Christians.* We cannot simply dismiss the Old Testament as *written for them.* So even though it is clear that the Torah/Law does not apply to Gentile Christians in the same way as it did to Jews who lived before the coming of Messiah, at some level the Old Testament is still written for *our* benefit. Even though it is clear that much of the prophetic material deals neither with general principles for a godly life nor with the coming of the Messiah, but rather with the specifics of life in the centuries before Christ, *it is still written for us.* What does that mean?

This is actually a huge question that we can't deal with adequately in this short chapter, but I think it must mean that, if we do it properly, it is perfectly valid to make applications from the Old Testament to us *as Christians.* We must always read forward from the Old Testament to Jesus *before* we make direct application to ourselves, but our work may not be finished there. If I can put it like this, the answer is not always *just* Jesus (even if I always want to preach 'the gospel' from this text).

Is the Old Testament moving towards Jesus? Yes, it is. Do I want people to walk away with a fresh sense of the power and grace that God has given us in Christ every time I open the Old Testament? Yes, I do. Is Jesus visible in every verse of the Old Testament? No, he isn't. If we pull back the camera far enough, eventually Jesus will come into view as the fulfilment of all that is going on. But sometimes we have to pull back quite a long way to see that. And, in the meantime, we ignore at our peril all the other stuff that is there.

So, for example, take Song of Songs. I do think that, ultimately, the Song does preach the gospel. But most of the book is about... yes, it's about sex. So do we ignore the sex because it doesn't fit into our biblical theological scheme very neatly? Do we do 'a Marcion' and cut out everything apart from the single allusion to God? No, we don't—at least not if we believe that this was written for us. Being committed to preaching the gospel from the Old Testament means that I must understand how this text is affected by the coming of Christ (as well as how this particular text launches us towards Christ—but we will see that below, when we look at biblical theology). But once I understand the gospel influence, I'm keen to know how the text is going to shape and inform my (Christian) life.

For human beings

There is a second level of reading the Bible in stereo that is easy to miss. The Bible—and the Old Testament in particular— was written for us as human beings. It's entirely possible to overplay the 'Jewishness' of the Old Testament.

Even the best biblical theologies often overlook the importance of Genesis 1-11 in setting the context for the Old Testament. Genesis 1-11 makes it clear that the Bible addresses the entire human race, and the call of Abraham depicts how God deals with all of humanity through one family. The repeated emphasis on Adam/new Adam theology through Genesis (and then through the rest of the Bible) underlines the way in which God works through one man to bless everyone who believes.

So while it is clear throughout the Old Testament that Israel is the chosen people of God, this one people also represents all people. Israel becomes the new Adam.[3] *At one level, then, many texts about Israel's response to God can be read as representative of all humanity's response to their creator.* Even though the details of their experience will differ greatly from our own, *their stupidity is our stupidity, their idolatry is our idolatry, their angst is our angst,* and so on. Israel, in a very real sense, represents us. They are 'priests' for the rest of humanity.

I've heard many sermons based on Old Testament passages that sound more like ancient history lectures than heart-changing messages from the living God because the preacher hasn't picked up this most basic connection. In the Old Testament we read about people like us—in fact, we read about people who *represent* us.

Just as a sermon's big idea bears repeating, so does this point: the Old Testament was written about them, but it is *for us.* Understanding and remembering this point will greatly enrich our preaching on the Old Testament as well as the New. If we read and preach the text in stereo, we will make clear that the passage in front of us is representative of our lives and struggles as human beings, and it addresses us as the people of God who are shaped and affected at the most profound level by the coming of Christ. Our preaching will instantly become richer and fuller and more engaging.

So that's step one (the hermeneutics). And step two? That's where biblical theology comes in.

---

3   For example, see Psalm 8 and the whole fabric of Ezekiel.

Finding a route to the gospel (or why biblical theology really matters)

The Bible has a storyline. This is obvious, I know, but it's absolutely crucial. It took Graeme Goldsworthy's masterful little book *Gospel and Kingdom* to point this out to many of us. Since its publication, Goldsworthy and many others have provided more great resources for getting to grips with the flow of biblical theology. So if you haven't read *Gospel and Kingdom,* or Vaughan Roberts' *God's Big Picture,* or Don Carson's *The God Who is There* or James Hamilton III's *God's Glory in Salvation through Judgement,* we'd recommend that you put this book down right now and come back to finish this chapter when you have. The idea that we need to read every part of the Bible in the light of the whole in order to understand its breadth and depth is so simple and yet absolutely fundamental. It would be counterproductive to continue any further without first getting a handle on this.

So (and welcome back to those of you who have been off for a biblical-theological-speed-read), why does this matter so much? Because if we're aiming to preach the gospel of Jesus from everywhere in the Bible, then we have to see that *the gospel of Jesus **is** everywhere in the Bible.*

Charles Spurgeon once said to a young preacher:

> Don't you know, young man, that from every town and every village and every hamlet in England, wherever it may be, there is a road to London? So from every text of Scripture there is a road to Christ. And my dear brother, your business is, when you get to a text, to say, now, what is the road to Christ? I have never found a text that had not got a road to Christ in it, and if ever I do find one, I will go over hedge and ditch but

> I would get at my Master, for the sermon cannot do
> any good unless there is a savour of Christ in it.[4]

I love that quotation—and Spurgeon got it absolutely right. If we read the Old Testament properly, then we'll see that every part of the Old Testament is pushing us steadily towards the gospel, which the New Testament unveils in all its glorious detail. There is indeed a legitimate route from every part of the Old Testament to the New. (Of course, enthusiastic preachers down through the years have also carved out plenty of illegitimate routes, but hopefully it will become clear by the end of this chapter why they're illegitimate.)

What are these routes? What does the network of connections that makes up biblical theology look like?

Don Carson has helpfully pointed out that there are around 20 *legitimate biblical-theological routes travelled by the apostles* from the Old Testament to the New. These routes, or 'trajectories', include:

- Creation
- Fall
- Covenant and promise
- Temple
- Sonship
- Exodus
- Messiah
- Resurrection
- Israel and the church[5]

---

4   CH Spurgeon, *The Soul Winner,* Christian Heritage, Fearn, 1995, p. 79.
5   DA Carson, in the Fall semester 2012-2013 syllabus for his *Biblical Theology and Interpretation* course at Trinity Evangelical Divinity School, email, 30 August 2012, pp. 3-5. Alongside these fairly obvious major trajectories are other minor (but nonetheless important) trajectories that contribute to the richness of biblical theology.

Presumably Jesus highlighted these on the road to Emmaus (Luke 24), which then launched the apostles on their own biblical theology project. Carson argues for a redemptive-historical model in which, like the apostles, we follow biblical trajectories from the Old Testament to the New. There is no surer way of finding the kind of route that Spurgeon talked about. I have yet to come across a richer model for handling the Bible as a whole than that proposed by Carson, Greg Beale and others.[6] Biblical theology is essentially that: looking for connecting themes that run right through the Scriptures and following them from one end to the other.

Goldsworthy does this in *Gospel and Kingdom* (where he follows the 'kingdom' trajectory), as does James Hamilton in *God's Glory in Salvation through Judgement*. Different theologians follow one or more of these trajectories all the way through the Bible. There is no single trajectory, however, that seems adequate to do justice to the wealth of Old Testament material (which explains why, for example, it can be so difficult to deal with wisdom literature—it might not be on the direct path of the particular trajectory that we are following). The reason there is more to be done in biblical theology is that the richness of the text demands it.

Phil likes to think about these connections and trajectories from a slightly different angle. (And because he's an engineer at heart, he's even drawn some diagrams for us.) In John 5:39-40, Jesus says to the Jews:

---

6   DA Carson and GK Beale (eds), *Commentary on the New Testament Use of the Old Testament,* Baker, Grand Rapids, 2007; GK Beale, *Handbook on the New Testament Use of the Old Testament,* Baker, Grand Rapids, 2012; BS Rosner, TD Alexander, G Goldsworthy and DA Carson (eds), *The New Dictionary of Biblical Theology: Exploring the unity and diversity of Scripture,* IVP, Downers Grove, 2004.

"You search the Scriptures because you think that in them you have eternal life; and *it is they that bear witness about me,* yet you refuse to come to me that you may have life."

In other words, although there was always a clear pathway through the Scriptures to Jesus and eternal life, plenty of Israelites found other pathways to alternate destinations like strict observance of the law, temple-based ritualism, ill-fated wars with the Romans, or weird end-time eschatologies. They branched off the only line leading to life.

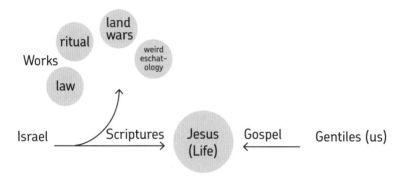

Now as Gentiles, we're only invited into those Old Testament Scriptures because we've *already* come to Jesus to have life. How foolish of us, then, to go back and study those Scriptures and find our destination anywhere else. Ultimately, our *interest*, and our *goal* and our *intention*, is to make our way from anywhere in the Old Testament back towards life in Christ… which is where we started.

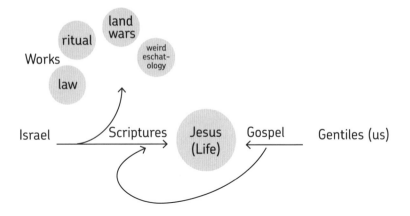

Some critics of biblical theology complain that it's built on a circular argument. Of course it is… it's an *a priori commitment* to preaching Christ rather than Old Testament legalism or Old Testament moralism or weird Old Testament prophecies that lead somewhere else. We *intentionally* preach Christ, finding any road we can—because Christ is where we have found life.

Our challenge, then, is to help people understand the flow of biblical theology. Because when people grasp the Bible's redemptive storyline, the power of God's word is unleashed and the Spirit uses it to change lives. How do we do this? We make sure that we connect what God has said in the Old Testament passage we are preaching from with what he has done for us in the Lord Jesus Christ. Then we explain what difference that makes in our lives. That's preaching the gospel of Jesus from everywhere. This includes, of course, articulating what we have to do to be saved. But it is so much more—as we explain what God has done for us in Christ to rescue us and enable us to live for him for our whole lives and beyond. But there is a very big danger in this approach.

A caution

As I have stumbled along, trying to preach the gospel of Jesus from everywhere and often bumping into things in my ignorance, not making the connections clear, I have come to realize one important thing. There is a difference between *doing biblical theology* and *preaching in a way that is shaped by biblical theology.* When I listen to you preach, do I want to see that you have grappled with the biblical theological implications of the text? Yes, I do. Do I want listening to a sermon to feel like sitting at home reading a book on biblical theology? No, I don't. There is a difference between *doing biblical theology* and *preaching in a way that is shaped by biblical theology.*

We need to work hard at understanding how the Old Testament text launches us towards Jesus. We need to get our heads around the range of trajectories, or themes, that we looked at above. That's biblical theology and, as we've seen, it's very important. But *the goal of every talk must **not** be to show people how this particular part of the Bible fits into biblical theology.* If we simply transfer our biblical theological insights into a sermon text, two things will happen. First, every sermon we preach from the Old Testament will sound and feel exactly the same. Second, we will lose and bore our listeners.

If, for example, we hop up every Sunday and, in an effort to make sure that we preach the Bible (and, I suppose, the Old Testament in particular) in its biblical theological context, we pause about halfway through and say something like, "Of course, to understand this text we need to go back to Genesis 1-3…" And then if we follow that up with a scenic tour all the way from Genesis to Revelation… well, many things could happen but they will probably not include lives transformed or hearts changed by the gospel.

So how do we preach in a way that is shaped by biblical theology?

How to preach the Old Testament using a biblical-theological approach

The Old Testament is not a biblical theology textbook; it is, essentially, 'preaching'. And though the entire Bible preaches the gospel message, it does so in immensely rich and varied ways. Much of this preaching clearly follows a redemptive-historical approach, but even within this structure there is great variety. In our preaching, therefore, we need to remember that *even when we know exactly where we're going, there are many ways to make the journey.*

It might help to think of it like this: if the trajectories that make up biblical theology are the roads and railways and flight paths that take us from A to B, we still have to decide how we're going to travel. There's a big difference between taking the highways and the back roads; or between travelling by train, plane and helicopter. As Fiona and I know, there is a huge difference between travelling as a family with kids (with regular stops to deal with vomiting, fighting and moaning), and travelling on our own! Knowing where we are going *doesn't mean every journey has to be exactly the same!*

So even though we're committed to biblical theology and know that there are about 20 main themes that connect the Old Testament to the New Testament through the work of Christ, we don't jump in the car every Sunday and drive at the same pace down the same roads enthusiastically pointing out the same landmarks. There are different ways to travel down various routes to appreciate numerous vistas as we travel to our destination.

Every journey from the Old Testament can feel and sound slightly different—depending on how quickly we travel, how often we stop, and who is in the back seat. There are at least nine different types of 'journey' we can take when preaching biblical theology, so let's unpack these various means of travel.[7] (And remember: this is not 'How to *do* biblical theology'; this is 'How to preach in a way that is *shaped by* biblical theology and doesn't bore the pants off people'.)

1. Follow the plan

It's possible to simply follow God's unfolding master plan through to its conclusion in Christ from almost any point in the Old Testament (and particularly from any point in a narrative section). This is, essentially, the approach described above—and it's a valid and important way of preaching the Old Testament. But, like any method, it can become boring and predictable and lose its power when we overuse it. Sermons that 'follow the plan' are most natural and effective when there is some kind of *forward momentum* in the text itself. So, for example, when preaching from Ruth 4, which traces Ruth's descendants as far as King David, or when explaining the story of Jehosheba in 2 Kings 11 where the same royal line is nearly wiped out, it would make perfect sense to follow the unfolding plan to its fulfilment in the Lord Jesus Christ.

2. Move to the fulfilment

When the passage from which we're preaching promises the perfect rescuing king, it might make more sense to move straight from the Old Testament to Christ than to focus on the way in which the plan unfolds. This approach is the equivalent

---

7   As we've said, biblical theology is looking for, and following, connecting themes that run through the Scriptures. I agree with Carson and Beale and others on this and am not proposing that we rearrange biblical theology into these categories. I am simply saying that these *ways of travelling* are suggested by the Old Testament itself.

of flying instead of driving the scenic route. So, for example, when looking at the 'king' laws of Deuteronomy 17, or the suffering of the servant in Isaiah 53, or Daniel's vision of the son of man in Daniel 7, there is no need to 'touch down' at multiple points en route to the fulfilment in Jesus. We can just take people straight to the heart of the gospel message.

3. Expose the problem

Many Old Testament texts don't explicitly refer to God's rescuer, or even to any plan to send one. Often the dominant note is human sinfulness (of individuals, of God's people, or of other nations). One powerful way to preach from these passages is to describe the problem the text highlights and then explain how Jesus is God's solution to that problem. So, for example, the text might train a spotlight on the inadequacy of the people God chooses to use (e.g. the proud and stubborn Moses in Exodus 6 or the licentious Samson in Judges 13-16), or on the fickleness of God's people (e.g. Exodus 32), or on their downright wickedness (e.g. Judges 21). In each case, it would be helpful to expose the nature of the problem—inadequate leaders, our inconsistency, our depravity—and show how God tackled these fundamental problems arising from human sinfulness in Jesus' death and resurrection. The end result is that the sermon takes on a problem-solution form, which sounds and feels different from sermons that follow the plan or move directly to the fulfilment. This variation in approach will enable listeners to understand and apply God's truth in a fresh way.

4. Highlight the (divine) attribute

One of the challenges of preaching Old Testament sermons is that long sections of the narrative and prophetic books are devoted to the wanton stupidity of God's people. And so 'exposing the problem' can become just as tired as 'following the plan'. One legitimate way of varying our approach to these passages is to shift the spotlight from *how we mess up* to *how God responds*. In other words, if we talk a little less about the problems we create, we can focus more on the God who is both willing and able to handle those problems. So, for example, it's not difficult to construct one sermon from Exodus 32-34 that focuses on the mess the people make and then to build another sermon around the fact that God is "the compassionate and gracious God, slow to anger, abounding in love and faithfulness" (Exod 34:6). Such an emphasis creates a natural connection for helping listeners to see this aspect of God's character even more clearly in the gospel. Similarly, God's patience and grace with his people are very evident in Judges 13-16—even when those people didn't really care about character issues. And in explaining the Moses narrative in Exodus 6, it would be perfectly legitimate to contrast Moses' own character with that of the God who has introduced himself to Moses and is commissioning him.

In many cases, finding a different 'mode of travel' is simply a matter of subtly shifting emphasis to ensure that our approach is fresh. And that's particularly important when working through longer sections of the Old Testament. Though the text is never boring, taking the same approach to it week after week *can* be. It is a great thing when God works through us to surprise people with what is in the Bible.

5. Focus on the action
Another option is to focus not on a particular attribute of God but rather on what God *does*. Although not substantially different from highlighting an aspect of God's character, it is a distinct approach.

So, for example, in the story of the plagues in Exodus 7-11, rather than simply explaining the fact that God is all-powerful, we could focus on *how* God defeats the powers of evil. Similarly, in the David and Goliath incident in 1 Samuel 17, I think the most natural way to deal with the text is to concentrate on the way in which God chooses to take on his enemies, which he then does in an even more obvious and decisive way on the cross (e.g. Col 2:15).

It is also perfectly legitimate and sometimes helpful to begin by focusing on what one or more of the human actors does in the narrative and then show how Jesus does the same thing on a grander, more effective scale in the New Testament. For example, Boaz's tenderness and kindness to Ruth (Ruth 2-3), wonderful as it is, pales in comparison to the tenderness and kindness Jesus demonstrates repeatedly throughout the Gospel narratives. This is not to say that the writer consciously prepared the way for Jesus in this text but that from our perspective— this side of the cross—similarities are clearly visible. It's useful to remember that people in the Old Testament at their best, while still being sinful, *can sometimes act like Jesus*.

6. Explain the category

The sixth distinct way of moving from the Old Testament text to the message of the gospel is not to focus on the action, or on what the passage shows us about the God and Father of our Lord Jesus Christ (which is then more fully revealed in the gospel), but rather to build the sermon around a key category. So, for example, rather than focusing on the promises made to Abraham or on how Isaac's survival was crucial to God's unfolding plan, a sermon on Genesis 22 could explore the whole idea of substitution, which is introduced and explained by this and a range of other key Old Testament texts. A sermon on Deuteronomy 20 might focus on God's justice, and God's faithfulness could take centre stage when preaching from Hosea 1 and 2. This is a more thematic approach, but it is (a) firmly anchored in the text; (b) controlled by the text; and (c) intended to shed light on the text rather than to launch into unrelated areas.

7. Point out the consequences

Sometimes, in Old Testament narrative in particular, it's helpful to concentrate on the consequences within the story itself of choosing obedience or disobedience. Almost the entire Old Testament canon operates within a framework of blessing and curse. (Deuteronomy 27-30 establishes this most clearly and the New Testament picks it up powerfully in, for example, 1 Corinthians 15 in Paul's 'Second Adam' section.) There are only two ways to live. This is a powerful way of explaining Joshua 7, for example, or the aftermath of the Bathsheba incident in 2 Samuel 12. Concentrating on consequences can also be extremely powerful when looking at the wisdom literature.

8. Describe the ideal human character

Passages that set out what it means to be godly can be some of the most difficult to handle in a way that does justice to the sweep of biblical theology. So, for example, in our fear of sounding legalistic, we often neglect passages like Psalm 1 or Proverbs 3 (and much of the wisdom literature), Micah 6:8, and the other prophetic passages that call us to act justly. The challenge is to find a way of teaching these passages that preserves their impact as well as their biblical-theological context.

How do we do that? One possibility is simply to describe the character of the godly man or woman that God is working to produce. This is basically Christlikeness, and anticipates what all God's people will be like in the new creation. These eschatological snapshots occur all through the Old Testament, in the teaching of Jesus (particularly in the Sermon on the Mount), and on through the New Testament. When we recognize that these are the very traits that the work of Jesus produces in his people, it ensures that our teaching even on these passages is gospel-filled and gospel-driven.

9. Satisfy the longing
Some passages in the Old Testament are charged with pain, disappointment and a longing for God to act. I would argue that the prayers of both Nehemiah 9 and Daniel 9 fall into this category, as does Nehemiah 13 and many of the psalms (this is a helpful way of preaching the troublesome Psalm 137, for example). These are examples of Old Covenant believers longing for the New Covenant (irrespective of how this is articulated). It is natural, then, after dealing with the frust-ration, anger or longing that's in the text, to move to the way in which these issues are resolved by the coming of Jesus to set up the new covenant.

Finally...
These nine pathways (and if you identify others, please tell me) all help to keep sermons on Old Testament passages centred on the gospel. The next time you're preaching a series on an Old Testament book, sit down and divide it into 'expository units' (see chapter 4 for more on how to define these units). Jot down what you think the big idea of each section is. Then note what you think might be the most effective and faithful way of moving from the text to the gospel. That's when this way of thinking comes into its own. When you're not using the

same well-trodden path every week, people will be surprised, encouraged, pointed to Jesus and made to gasp at the gospel—rather than being bored.

However, it's important to remember that these pathways are just 'scaffolding'—they're useful during construction but should never be left in place once the work is done. We should never use the words, "And now I'm following the plan" or "Today we'll be focusing on the action" in our sermons. These pathways, or categories, are simply aids *for us as we prepare*—we don't need to explain them to our listeners. They help us to write the sermon, but they shouldn't appear in it.

It's also important to remember that these are not watertight theological categories; rather, they remind us of the way that biblical theology works and prompt us to fresh thinking. They suggest approaches to preaching that *flow out of the text itself* rather than being imposed from elsewhere. When you know the incredible destination to which you're headed (the truth of the gospel), the last thing you want to do is get stuck in a particular biblical-theological rut along the way.

So our aim is *to preach in a way that is shaped by biblical theology*. This requires doing the hard work of hermeneutics and biblical theology and then crafting a message that conveys the big idea of the passage in a clear and engaging way so that our listeners can apply God's truth to their lives.

Once we have done that, all we have left to do is stand and deliver.

6

Stand and deliver

L IKE F EDE X OR A GOOD obstetrician, preachers deliver. Week after week we face up to our fears, rise to our feet in front of a not-so-crowded church, and speak.

And here's where the rubber hits the road. Here's where you'll either spur people into life or put them to sleep. A lot depends on the work you've already done in preparation—are you ready to be concise and crystal clear? A lot depends on your heart—are you passionate, excited by the gospel, enthused by your passage, and in love with the church the Lord Jesus has put under your care? If you're just going through the motions, it will show.

But a lot also depends on the skills and habits that contribute to your *verbal energy*—the ingredients of vitality and verve that either enliven or eviscerate the same words from the lips of two different speakers.

Sometimes we call it 'personality'—the charisma, warmth, or charm that makes or breaks the careers of presidential candidates, TV anchors and megachurch pastors alike. But what exactly is it?

I call it a 'zing' thing. But Gary says 'zing' is not in his dictionary and I need to define it. Give me a break! *You* know what I mean, don't you? It's… intangible. It's zest and freshness and energy. You know it when you meet it. The communication zing I'm talking about comes from deep reserves of intelligence and graciousness and humour and wisdom. This zing doesn't just shape the words; it also shapes the way the words are spoken. The act of delivery. The pitch, the pace, the punch… the perfectly placed pauses. That's a lot of 'p' words.

So how do I get zing? I gave up the hope of making it as a megachurch preacher years ago—but, for the sake of keeping my current crowd of victims awake, can I somehow become a more engaging, interesting and energized 'me'?

As starting point, here's some advice I heard twice in the same week, both times from visual designers. It started me thinking. In *The Non-Designers Design Book*, Robin Williams says the secret of attention-grabbing graphic design is **contrast**. Make the bold ***really* bold**. Make visual contrasts that jump off the page. Her advice? "Don't be a wimp!"[1]

Exactly the same advice came two days later from an interior designer working on our bathroom renovation plans. "Don't be wimps", Katie said. No lame half-measures or bland

---

1   R Williams, *The Non-Designer's Design Book,* 2nd edn, Peachpit Press, Berkeley, 2004, p. 63. If you're pastoring a church, take a closer look at your weekly bulletin and see how it rates. It's probably bland. And features Comic Sans along with seven other fonts. *The Non-Designers Design Book* is well worth a look.

colours. Be definite; make a statement, not an apology. (Thanks, Katie. The new bathroom looks great!)

So what happens when we try to muscle-up the contrast in our preaching? Could you (in your wildest dreams) be more vividly emphatic without crossing over into corny? Louder without sounding aggressive, then softer without being silent? Could you talk faster than ever before, then more deliberately than you've ever dreamed possible… without making people laugh? Preachers like Bill Hybels, Mark Driscoll and Tim Keller do this incredibly well, which is one of the reasons they're downloaded millions of times each week.

Of course, context always counts. If you're preaching to 20 people in a small room, you'll be more constrained than on a large stage. But the same advice still applies… don't be a wimp! You'll need to paint in bolder colours and broader brushstrokes than you expect just to keep people awake.

The delivery sphere

So, let's take a few steps back and think about the mechanics of delivery. You've worked hard at your exegesis, and distilled your passage to a clear and driving 'big idea' that you've used to frame a compelling sermon. Well done. But then you stand up to speak, and your normally vibrant personality suddenly deflates like an empty balloon. Now is the time to remember… don't be a wimp!

Here's where I find it useful to think about the 'delivery sphere'. Imagine that balloon, still inflated and see-through, a bubble in space and time. If you can remember your high school math class, picture the x, y and z axes, and label them pace, volume and pitch. Great. Now we've got a 3D mental playground, and you can see that any point within that space represents a different mix of the three variables that describe the way someone is speaking.

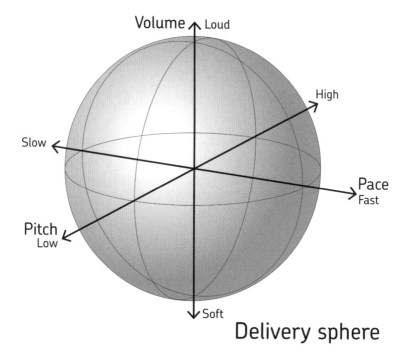

Delivery sphere

Now imagine tracing a line around that space that follows the trajectory of a preacher. It's a deliberate start, perhaps—slow and soft. The speed picks up to a climactic moment that's fast and loud. Then the pitch drops as the pace slows to create a sombre tone… can you picture the trail?

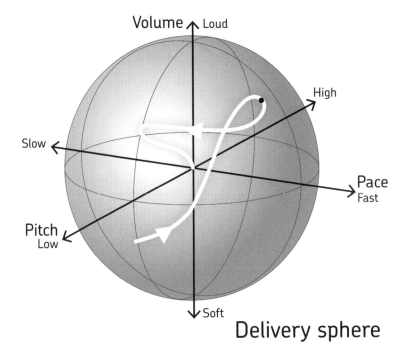

Volume — Loud
High
Slow
Pace — Fast
Pitch — Low
Soft

Delivery sphere

Now here's where the mental picture becomes useful. Imagine that speaker is you. Imagine again that you're tracing that line around inside the bubble that defines the entire pitch, pace and volume space that's at your disposal. The outer reaches of the space are the points as high and low as you can possibly pitch your voice, as fast and slow as you can possibly speak, and as loud as you can yell and as soft as you can whisper. These are places you've only visited in the rarest moments of passion. But they exist.

Now take yourself somewhere private and hit 'record' on your phone while you dry-run a sermon. Listen back and track yourself around the delivery sphere. How much of that giant-sized bubble of potential are you using? My guess is not nearly as much as you could be.

Better still, if you have someone who's willing to listen to you, make a copy of the diagram at the end of appendix 2 and ask them to plot the line they hear as you deliver your sermon. (It's kind of tricky to draw a 3D plot on a piece of paper, so they'll need to use their imagination… but they'll soon get the idea.) I have to warn you that you'll feel kind of dumb while you're doing it—but don't let that confine your delivery! Abandon your natural embarrassment. It's worth the pain. (If the prospect seems too daunting to you, try coming back to this idea after you read chapter 7, 'Faithful wounds'.)

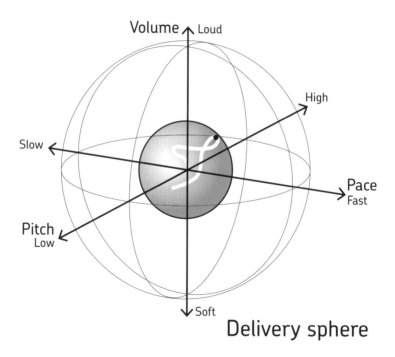

Delivery sphere

How fast did you talk? How slowly? What's the pitch of your normal, conversational voice? Did it change? When you're passionate or excited, do you speak louder? How much louder? If you've got extra range at your disposal, when do you use it?

Dull preaching shares a few characteristics. Monotone delivery—locked on a fixed pitch—is hypnotic. Delivery that's too slow is deadly too. Mark Driscoll typically clocks in at a lively 175 words per minute. Gary Millar cracks along at an average 167 wpm, Tim Keller varies between 162 and 177, and I'm usually hovering around the 135 words per minute mark, with bursts of up to 167 balanced by pensive patches at around 108. Interestingly, neither Driscoll nor Keller sound rushed—just energized. And Gary, though decidedly Irish, is a delight to listen to.

In the example of your own preaching that you just recorded (or your honest mental self-audit), was there even the slightest audible hint of energy and passion? Was there any contrast? Any drama? Or just small brush strokes and bland colours? Take the hint. Mentally expand your preaching sphere. Go where you've never been before. Explore the contrasts, and don't be a wimp!

Agile delivery

After spending hours with my preaching classes trying to analyse and measure speakers like Mark Driscoll and Tim Keller, I have to admit that I'm still trying to figure out what makes them so listenable. Driscoll and Keller, for example, have completely different styles. Yet they're both equally—and instantly—compelling. And again, while their reputations are built around content and not style, I suspect either of them could hold an audience while they described paint drying.

Driscoll is a master at using the extremes of the delivery sphere. But that's only part of the story. I'm beginning to think that *agility* in moving around that imaginary space is one of the defining marks of an energizing communicator.

My son-in-law gave me a miniature quadrotor helicopter for Christmas. So far I've failed dismally to navigate it—in fact, I'm about to visit my neighbour to retrieve it from his back garden. But it's fascinating to watch these high-tech toys in the hands of a computer scientist like Vijay Kumar, who used a fleet of quadrotors to demonstrate agile navigation programming in a recent TED talk.[2]

Kumar explained that we've been taught to think about movement in simple terms. We call the rate of change of distance over time *speed*, and the rate of change of speed is called *acceleration*. But what do you call the rate of change of acceleration? And the rate of change of that? Physicists call them 'jolt' and 'snap', respectively. Kumar demonstrated how, when you start factoring those third and fourth derivatives into your navigation algorithms, you end up with a copter that's incredibly agile.

Here's the point. Watching a snappy programmed quadrotor in action gives me the same thrill as listening to Mark Driscoll in full flight. And so it got me speculating that maybe the best natural communicators are working at that level. It's not just about fine-tuning our delivery pitch or pace or volume. What sets these people apart is their agility in moving from one point to another... the snap, the jolt, the agility of delivery that conveys underlying passion and adds that elusive zing.

When you try speaking like that, which I urge you to do, you'll find it takes a huge amount of energy. But it's exactly *that energy* that's transmitted to your listeners. It's contagious. In short, when it comes to sermon delivery, it's not just your *range* of volume, pitch and speed that counts—it's your *agility* in moving between modes. The drama in your delivery is all about in-flight dynamics. It's hard work, and to make progress you'll need to lose your natural inhibitions and fly a little. But

2   V Kumar, 'Robots that fly... and cooperate', TED talk, February 2012 (see especially from 6:00): www.ted.com/talks/vijay_kumar_robots_that_fly_and_cooperate.html

if you keep working at it, you'll find it eventually becomes more natural.

Purposeful delivery

How you craft your delivery doesn't just keep your listeners awake (important as that is). Agile delivery also drives home your big idea. Emphasis comes from contrast—from increasing and lowering your volume. The more sudden the change, the more it grabs the attention. You can emphasize a point by lowering your tone or by raising it, or even by inserting a deliberate pause…

But the question is this: how do you know *what* to emphasize? How do you decide when it's time for a crescendo? Or a burst of speed?

If you have a big idea, the answer is easy. You want to lead people through the logic of your sermon's big idea. Your progression towards the main point of your sermon shapes the way you emphasize every word and sentence you speak. Maybe you start with a light introduction to draw people in. Tread lightly. Next you recap some background. Move quickly, or you'll bog down your listeners. Now, though, you've reached A. Major. Building. Block. In. Your. Logic. Being punctiliar can be punchy. As your big idea—the one that's been gripping you since you first caught on to it at your desk on Thursday morning—drives you through the delivery of your sermon, you'll know when you're approaching the climax and you'll know instinctively how to deliver it.

Of course, if you're just *delivering* a string *of* disconnected ideas, you may as *well* just *emphasize* randomly. Listening to preaching like that is like travelling on a bumpy road.

To smooth the journey, one simple technique that I still use is to write the words I intend to emphasize in UPPERCASE.

But take care. Nothing loses listeners more than random or misplaced emphasis—and I hear young preachers do it regularly. It's worth planning ahead so that your emphasis builds a chain of meaning... a trail of breadcrumbs that takes your listeners exactly where you want them to go.

Here's the goal: make sure you're totally sold on the big idea of your sermon. Make sure you're driven by it. Then you'll know how to say the things you say, because they will come from a heartfelt passion. This doesn't mean, however, that you can forget about adding the zing. If you're the shy type, you'll have to amplify your passion and deliberately bounce around the delivery sphere. It's only when you get outside your normal kitchen-conversation comfort zone that people will start to notice that you mean business. It's all about *owning your words*—using the words you've prepared to communicate the *big idea of your passage in a way that moves people towards faith and obedience.*

My last word on delivery? All I can say is that this stuff takes energy. It takes a firm resolve as you stand up to speak, and stamina to keep pushing through. It takes energy to raise your volume and lower it, to pick just the right pitch and pace. It takes energy to emphasize your point and to demand the attention of your listeners and hold on to it. It takes energy to turn sharp corners in full flight. But that's exactly the point. Because that's the energy you transmit to your listeners. And it might even keep them awake.

7

Faithful wounds:
the importance of critique

Pain, pain and more pain

Getting feedback on my preaching is just about the worst thing there is. It's about as desirable as having pins stuck in my eyes. And then there's the bad news—it doesn't get any more pleasant as the years go by (sorry to depress you if you're starting out, but I think it actually gets worse!). And yet there is probably nothing more important for anyone who teaches the Bible than loving, godly, perceptive criticism.

Over the years, I've thought long and hard about why I find it so painful to receive feedback (either before or after preaching). Sadly, I think there's only one answer. Sin. If you are a pastor/teacher, you will be tempted (at least from time to time) to try to find your identity and significance in your preaching. I know that I'm particularly vulnerable to sinning like this when things are going badly in other areas of my life. So when I'm feeling that I'm a rubbish husband, an inept father, a selfish friend and an incompetent leader, I am sorely tempted to say to myself, "Well, at least I can preach!" Not only is this ungodly (for all kinds of reasons), it is also stupid. Because it means that when anyone (usually my wife, Fiona) points out the obvious (and sometimes ridiculous) flaws in what I have just inflicted (or was planning to inflict) on unsuspecting people, my world virtually collapses.

And the fact that it all matters so much just makes it worse. If we believe that God, through the Spirit, changes people through Bible teaching, and that teaching the Bible clearly and well is the primary responsibility of pastor/teachers, and that ministry is essentially about word ministry, then all that adds a further layer of intensity to conversations about why the sermon isn't, or wasn't, up to par. But this is one of those times when there's no gain without pain.

The importance of peer review

Over the years I've become increasingly aware that I need people in my life (in addition to my wife) who aren't afraid to say, "Gary, that was really poor" or, "Brother, I'm sorry to tell you that you really missed the point". But those kinds of relationship don't come easily. We need to develop relationships with a few people whom we can trust—people who not only share our theological vision and our basic commitments about preaching, but who are also skilled at highlighting where we are prone to going wrong, and who are not afraid to say so in a loving, godly way. I suspect that a minority of preachers have these kinds of relationships.

At Queensland Theological College we are actively encouraging students to form small preaching groups *that will continue to meet long after they leave college.* The format of these groups is very simple. Before we meet, we all listen to a sermon preached recently by one of the members *in a local church* (so that we are listening to the 'real thing', not a presentation to peers). When we meet, we give feedback and we pray together. Over the course of five or six weeks everyone gets 'critiqued' (including me), and over the course of their time at college real trust develops between members of these groups. My dream is that, in the years ahead, every QTC graduate in a teaching ministry will be part of one of these groups.

You may not have that kind of group in place—but you really need to be part of one. We all do.

What we need most

Appendix 2 contains the sermon feedback form that Phil uses in our preaching course at QTC. It's really useful and a great place to start when seeking, and giving, loving, godly feedback. In chapter 8 and appendix 1 you will find examples of sermons and mutual sermon critiques by Phil and me, using this feedback sheet, so you can see how this valuable process works in practice.

But let's look now at the needs that are most pressing for all of us who preach regularly. We need people who will pull us up on these particular temptations.

Getting the big idea wrong/not preaching the passage

Those of us who have been preaching for a while are more likely to think that we have moved beyond the possibility of simply getting the text wrong (or, worse, sidelining the text to air our own particular vital insight for that week). We need people to check that we are handling the text properly. Those who are just starting out, on the other hand, need a mentor to help establish and maintain the discipline of getting the big idea every time we preach. As we've seen, there is a learning curve and it takes practice.

Self-indulgence
One of the dangers for preachers is that many of us are prone to falling in love with the sound of our own voices. It can become 'all about me' if we are wallowing in our own suffering for the gospel or if we are relishing the power and attention. When this begins to happen, we start talking more and more about ourselves and are less and less concerned about the impact of what we are saying on those who are listening.

Not preaching the gospel
We shouldn't have to say it, but it happens. Every so often, we leave what God has done in Jesus on our desks at home, and slip into telling people what *they really need to do*. This most often occurs when we're angry with people, but it can happen anytime. When it does, we need someone to point it out to us—quickly.

Not preaching the gospel to people's hearts
We need to preach in a way that gets under people's skin, by negotiating obstacles that might stop them from listening (e.g. tiredness, over-familiarity, a sense that this doesn't apply to them, etc.). We also need to preach in a way that applies the gospel to their hearts, engaging them with the real issues they face and moving and enabling them (by the Spirit) to live for Jesus (as we discussed in chapter 2). That's what God calls us

to do—and that's why I want to know if I've left people cold or even bored. If I've done great exegesis and preached a sermon packed full of insights that has no 'so what' to it, I need to know.

Insensitivity

Sometimes we lose the plot in terms of applying the text winsomely and tenderly to the whole range of people in our church family. Sometimes we say insensitive things. Or when we move into a new stage of life we forget what it's like to be a teenager, or single, or struggling to cope with young kids. And chances are we won't still be preaching when we finally understand what it's like to be elderly and facing end-of-life concerns. Sometimes we say stupid things. And somebody needs to tell us.

Trying to be too clever

Another temptation, especially when we spend so much time reading, is to try to be clever. We might come across some great insight of our own (or, more likely, someone else's great insight) and decide that we need to inflict it on a congregation (just in case they might have forgotten how brilliant we are). Again, if this is happening we need someone to tell us so that we can repent and pray harder for humility and wisdom.

There are always other temptations, of course, but I think this list covers most of the broad categories. We need to remember that all of these 'mistakes' are *sin*. There is a sad irony in the fact that many of us who are so quick to say (and preach) with JC Ryle that "a right understanding of sin lies at the root of all saving Christianity",[1] are also very slow to acknowledge that our

1   JC Ryle, *Holiness*, ReadaClassic.com, Cedar Lake, 2011, p. 15.

preaching 'gaffes' are actually deeply sinful. To miss the point of a passage because we have decided that what we want to say is more important than what God has to say is sinful. To abuse the privilege of preaching by talking about ourselves or by trying to make ourselves seem witty or 'in' or 'hip' is just plain sinful. Not preaching the gospel of grace but pushing people back to legalism is ultimately—yes, sinful. And so it goes on.

What we need most as preachers is to apply the gospel to ourselves—to the motivation, content and manner of our preaching. Often what we need to do in response to critique is not to try harder. Rather, we need to repent and run back into the arms of Jesus whom we preach.

On the receiving end—taking feedback well

Fiona and I once had a conversation with Phillip Jensen about how best to offer critique. He suggested (with a straight face) that Fiona should never offer any feedback on a sermon I'd preached until at least Tuesday morning. He explained that preachers feel too raw and vulnerable after preaching, and then many take Monday as a day off, so Tuesday was good. When we asked if his wife, Helen, waited until Tuesday, Phillip grinned and said, "You must be joking!" But that's the balance we need to seek.

On the one hand, giving a sermon is spiritually and physically draining. (If you find that it's not, you should probably re-read chapter 6, 'Stand and deliver'!) So feedback is always hard to take immediately afterward. But on the other hand, the truth we preach is so important, and so much is at stake, that we can't possibly wait around for just the right moment to arrive. (Body language generally gives us some idea of what's coming by way of critique anyway—even if the words lag behind.)

I really do only have two pieces of advice on this:

1. Feedback *before* is painful, but it is less painful (and less guilt-inducing) than feedback *after*—so seek out feedback before you preach, if you possibly can.
2. Remember that feeding the people of God matters much more than your ego.

As Phil has worked with preaching trainees, he's been passionate about the value of 'feedback before'. He always works through the preach-and-critique process with trainees well before they preach in churchcs. Phil explains:

> For one thing, it helps objectify the draft version of the sermon. We can preach the draft to each other and hear how it sounds. We can work on the logic and check for natural style and clarity. It's one of the biggest benefits of working with a scripted sermon— you get a chance to improve on the draft.

Not only that, but because the preacher hasn't yet 'gone live' with the congregation, there's less sensitivity and less risk of hurt feelings. Phil says:

> The critique can be more robust, and most often there's a sense of gratitude, and a feeling that there's been substantial progress. When I've worked this way with our trainees at church, they'll always get frustrated by the time we're working through the third or fourth draft. But by Sunday, instead of a critique it's almost always a celebration.

As I've said, a degree of frustration and hurt feelings is inevitable. If you are the 'critiquer', you need to focus on being clear, loving and gentle without shirking from saying the hard things that sometimes need to be said. You also need to constantly examine your motivations for what you are choosing to say. If you are the 'critiquee', you need to resist the temptation to defend or justify yourself or feel sorry for yourself (or attack the critiquer). Instead, think of the people of God and the honour of Jesus. As John Chapman always used to say, the first 50 years are the hardest!

The long drive to Howth (A word to those who are married)

There is a stretch of road in Ireland that, for me, will always be synonymous with sermon critique—or, to be more accurate, sermon reconstruction or resuscitation. From 2000 to 2012, I was the pastor of a pair of Presbyterian churches in North Dublin. Every Sunday for 12 years, Fiona and I drove the 20 minutes between these churches after I had preached the first time and before I preached the second. Some Sundays, this seemed the longest road in Ireland.

Over the years, we have learned that it is less painful for me (and of greatest benefit to those who will hear the sermon) if I talk with Fiona all the way through the 'creative process'. I talk with her about the big idea of the passage, show her an outline and then ask her to read the script once I have a full draft. When we follow that process, we work together really effectively (and with the least pain). When we don't have that interaction, it's either because I'm not organized or because I'm unwilling to be vulnerable with a sermon with which I'm struggling (both of which, I realize, are sinful). Fiona, in addition to being spiritually perceptive and sensitive to hypocrisy and pretentiousness, has an uncanny ability to put her finger on what's wrong with a sermon. She is also a high school English teacher who runs the debating program in our local junior school, which means that she's a huge help to me at all kinds of levels in my preaching. Sadly, on those weeks when I was disorganized or too caught up in nursing my own pride to talk with her before Sunday morning, I deprived our church family of being helped by Fiona's selfless and invisible input and inflicted a sermon that was much worse than it needed to be on the first congregation—and we had a painful conversation on the long road to Howth. On those journeys the question was whether I could stop being defensive and feeling sorry for myself and start praying and thinking like mad to ensure that the second 'run through' was better.

Those of us who are married do have to find some way of working out the unique circumstances of being 'one flesh' with one of the people to whom we regularly teach the Bible. One person who is listening each Sunday has far more invested in (and is more affected by) our preaching than anyone else. Our marriages are inevitably bound up, at least to some degree, with the realities of ministry. It is a blessing and privilege to have a partner who works, cares, cries, rejoices and reflects with us. And we need to think and pray hard about the best ways to work together and support each other.

Some of us are not married. Some of us have spouses who are our best critics. Others of us have found that our marriages are healthier when we can maintain clearer boundaries between family and ministry. We are all different, and there is no perfect template, but the crucial point is that we seek and receive feedback on our preaching from someone on a regular basis.

Where do you begin?

Perhaps you've never done this or are in a situation where you don't yet have people in your life who could offer such feedback. If this is the case, depending where you're located, you could contact one of the following organizations:

- the Simeon Trust (US)[2]
- the Proclamation Trust (UK)[3]
- the Irish Preachers Conference[4]
- Cornhill Sydney.[5]

They all offer preaching workshops in which participants have the opportunity to offer and receive feedback on sermons in a collegial, supportive environment. You could also organize a small group of peers to do this and—and to pray for one another.[6]

If you're still wondering exactly what this kind of feedback looks like, read on. In the next chapter, Phil builds a sermon that I critique in appendix 1. We're both so convinced of the importance of peer review that we agreed to include our sermons, and our mutual critiques, in this book.

---

2   www.simeon.org
3   www.proctrust.org.uk
4   www.irishpreachers.org
5   www.cornhillsydney.com.au
6   You could even begin by reading and discussing this book together.

8

Let's build a sermon
Phil walks through the process of writing last Sunday's sermon

WHEN YOU'RE WRITING a book like this one, it's tempting to use your best-ever sermon as a model. But I figure it's more honest to share the sermon I'm working on right now, in real time. It's the last Sunday of the year and I'm scheduled to preach on Acts 8. Because many of our regulars are on vacation, we're combining our two morning congregations. It's Friday, I'm at my desk, and so far it just isn't coming together.

For starters, while Acts 8 is a simple and dynamic narrative, it's full of complex issues. Philip is preaching to the Samaritans. He performs remarkable miracles. The Samaritans are baptized, but only in the name of Jesus—why doesn't the Spirit come? (I'm reading FF Bruce's article on the question,[1] I'm looking at similar episodes through Acts, and I'm still perplexed.) And the apostles! Why are they still in Jerusalem when Jesus told them back in Acts 1:8 that it was *their* job to preach to Judea and Samaria and to the ends of the earth? Then there's Simon the Sorcerer, who raises a pile of questions of his own. And there's the Ethiopian eunuch. How do you explain what *that* means on a Sunday when the kids are still in church? And what's his connection with the rest of the chapter?

You're probably thinking that I've bitten off more than I can chew. Maybe that's material for three sermons. And you may be right. But as I follow the Ethiopian's reference back to Isaiah 53, there's a glimmer of light. Isn't it Isaiah who's just said that when the Lord's servant comes, "*All the ends of the earth* will see the salvation of our God" (52:10)?[2] The same Isaiah who says, "You will summon *nations you know not*" (55:5) a few chapters later? In fact, this is the prophet who is about to say:

> Let no *foreigner* who is bound to the LORD say,
> "The LORD will surely exclude me from his people."
> And let no *eunuch* complain,
> "I am only a dry tree." (Isa 56:3)

At this point, I'm thinking that maybe the integrating idea of the chapter is staring me in the face. I've been through my usual discipline of hand-writing the passage in two columns, but I've

---

1 FF Bruce, 'Luke's presentation of the Spirit in Acts', *Criswell Theological Review,* vol. 5, no. 1, 1990, pp. 15-29.
2 All Scripture quotations in this chapter are from the New International Version (2011 edition).

been so startled by the drama of Simon the Sorcerer and my own theological questions about baptism that I've failed to notice that the Samaritans (who are mentioned time and time again) are actually 'foreigners'. Alienated cousins of Israel, they were treated with disdain. Like the Ethiopian eunuch, who was only ever allowed as far as the temple car park, these Samaritans are most unlikely friends for Jewish Christians. And yet Philip preaches to them… and they believe.

By now I'm convinced that this is the idea that makes Acts 8 preachable as a unit. (If you're not sure that 'preachable' is a word, it probably means you've never had the 'aha' experience of finding an integrating idea!) The inclusion of Samaritans and an African eunuch starts a movement that brings together all kinds of unlikely friends in a way that even our church today should reflect. Is this happening? Are we welcoming all kinds of people because the Suffering Servant brought righteousness for all the nations? Are members of our 9 am congregation even prepared to mix with the rowdy crowd of strangers from 10.30 am? These are big questions, and I'm actually starting to feel them 'in my gut'. I'd love our church to be more like this, I'd love to be more like it myself—and I want to talk about it.

That means I'm ready to start working on a sermon. First, I need an introduction that raises the idea of *unlikely friendships*. Let's try this. (Reader alert: We're about to switch into that awkward 'speaking style' I warned about in chapter 6.[3] From this point on, don't expect a smooth read. See the cues for my PowerPoint slides, too.)

---

3   For greater readability, the words I usually put into UPPERCASE for emphasis (see chapter 6) are in **bold** here.

Acts 8: Unlikely Friendships[4]

Over our holidays Lou and I finally caught up with *Downton Abbey* on **DVD**. We're loving it. And can't wait for **series 3** on **TV**.

If you're not a *Downton Abbey* **fan**, or if you've never seen it, let me tell you, it's **not as bad as it sounds**.

It's a series that traces the lives of one **aristocratic family** and their **servants** through the huge cultural upheaval of **World War I**. And now beyond.

From a time when **lords were lords** and **ladies were ladies**. When the **kitchen maid** was **never to be seen upstairs**. When everybody **knew their place**. Through the **terrible**; or so it seemed. Through the **terrible changes** brought about by the **war**. And by **women wanting to vote**. And the **Irish wanting their freedom**.

▶ **[SLIDE Sybil and Branson]**

And worst of all, if you're **Lord Crawley**… is that his daughter **Lady Sybil**… **falls in love with Branson the chauffeur**. And without wanting to spoil the story too much… they **run off to Ireland and get married**.

Which again is a… it's a category, it's a whole way of thinking… that just **doesn't seem possible**. It's a **cultural divide** if you're **Lord Crawley**, that just **seems insurmountable**. A dividing line between people, between **types of people**… that just shouldn't and couldn't be crossed.

4   I preached this sermon at Mitchelton Presbyterian Church, Brisbane, on 30 December 2012. If you'd rather listen to this sermon (broad Aussie accent and all), you can find the audio and a video here: www.savingeutychus.com/resources

Now it's into a situation like that that we're coming this morning in the book of Acts. And one that if you stop to think about it, you'll see there's a line being crossed, in fact a number of lines, that you'll be **glad have been crossed**. Because you and I as it turns out are the ones from the **wrong side of the tracks**.

Now if you've never seen an episode of the very British TV show *Downton Abbey,* that opening might leave you cold. But I've tried to build in enough context to make sense of the fact that it's all about barriers being broken down, and the forming of 'unlikely friendships'. It's building a bridge—especially for fans of the show—with one footing firmly planted in life *now* (in front of the TV set), and another back in Acts 8. We're on our way.

Next, we'll need a brief recap of past weeks in our series in Acts, which week by week has been building on the theme of the worldwide authority of the ascended Jesus. Here's how I'll do it...

But the point is, and it's one the **first Christians are slow to learn**, the point is that the **kingdom of the King Jesus Christ who rules at the right hand of God** as we saw last week is a **kingdom** for **all the world**.

For all kinds of people. From all kinds of backgrounds. All brought together under **one king**.

The one who fulfils that ancient prophecy of Daniel—the son of man who'll **rule over every tongue and every tribe and every nation** at God's right hand.

And you'll remember **that's the mission** given first and foremost to the **apostles**. By Jesus himself. Back at the start of the book. Chapter 1 verse 8. Not just a **mission to Israel**. But to **everywhere**. Here's how he puts it:

▶ [SLIDE Acts 1:8]

"But you will receive power when the **Holy Spirit comes on you;** and **you will be my witnesses** in Jerusalem, and in all Judea **and Samaria, and to the ends of the earth."**

> Did you notice? There's lots of repetition there, partly because we're moving to a new thought. If I want people to move through the logical turning point with me, it's important to say the same thing at least three times to bring them with me. Logically, a 'kingdom for all the world' is going to include all kinds of people from all kinds of backgrounds. Logically, the gospel is going to include Judea and Samaria on its way to the 'ends of the earth'. And, having made the point, I want to show—and read aloud—the words of Jesus from Acts 1:8.
>
> The problem is, of course, that up to this point in Acts the mission has stalled in Jerusalem, and it's only now—because of persecution—that the gospel finally starts breaking boundaries. I'll say it this way:

Now **so far** in the book of Acts, all the action's been in **Jerusalem.** I don't know if you've noticed, in fact, **we usually don't. We** tend to read the Bible like it's **always about us.** But **so far**… so far in the gospel accounts, so far here in the book of Acts, so far **all the action has been Jewish.** With non-Jews like ourselves hardly getting a **look in.**

The **Jewish apostles**… filled with **God's Spiri.** The crowds of **Jews;** hearing them preach. The growing **church of Jews.** Hanging off every word of the teaching of the **apostles.** Amazed by the **signs and wonders** the apostles were doing among them. And most especially, **all of them**… Jewish. **Finally enjoying the gift of the Holy Spirit** so long ago promised. **To change their hearts.** So they're finally at last **tuned to living for God.**

All Jewish. Right up to chapter 8.

Even though Jesus had **said to them** before he left them, that **Jerusalem was just the starting point.**

Look at his words. See, he's the **son of man** who's going to **rule a kingdom not just of Israel**. But men and women from **every nation**. And so they're going to be witnesses…

In Jerusalem. In all Judea and Samaria. And to the **ends of the earth**.

And yet… right up to the stoning of Stephen… everything so far has been happening in **Jerusalem**.

And at last, here at the start of chapter 8, **it changes**. For the **most unlikely reason**. We're picking up right after the **stoning of Stephen**. And look what happens… chapter 8 verse 1.

▶ **[SLIDE Acts 8:1]**

> On that day a great persecution broke out against the church in Jerusalem, and **all except the apostles** were scattered **throughout Judea and Samaria**.

To be honest, I'd be surprised (and very grateful) if you actually bothered to read that section. The redundancy, the repetition, the short sentences that aren't even sentences. ("All Jewish." Give me a break—that's not a sentence!) But trust me. That's the pace of information flow that most people can comfortably take on board as *listeners* rather than readers.

So we've set the scene. We've arrived (at last) at chapter 8, we're on the edge of the Samaritan mission with the key phrase *"Judea and Samaria"*. We're almost ready to dive into the narrative. It's time to break out the present-tense verbs and try to breathe some new life into history. I'm going to very purposefully move into the 'narrative *now*' that places us right in the action. I'll emphasize the key present tense indicators in italics to help you spot them.

Even then it's **odd isn't it**.

Even *now*, the **apostles**, who Jesus directly **told to go to Judea** and **Samaria** and the **ends of the earth**… *are* for some reason **still staying put in Jerusalem**.

I mean, maybe *they're* **slow learners**. But whatever the reason, **the *gospel's* going to keep going**.

And in the end *it's* another one of the **food management guys**, another one of the **care team guys** like **Stephen**… who *takes* the historic step.

So while *they're* **mourning** for Stephen, verse 2, and *Saul's* **systematically destroying the church**, verse 3, you'll see that **Philip**—along with everyone else who's been scattered —*they're* preaching **the word** wherever they *go*.

Which is exactly where Jesus had **said to go**. Judea. **And Samaria**.

I could have more correctly said, "Even *then*, the apostles *were* still staying put in Jerusalem… maybe they *were* slow learners… it *was* another one of the food management guys… who *took* the historic step… they *preached* the word wherever they *went*." But that just sounds so… past. Doesn't it?

In terms of the logic of the sermon, I'm thinking at this point that I need to reinforce the tension over the inclusion of Samaria. Too little work at this point, and there's nothing to marvel over at the end. That means I'll need a little Old Testament background, and maybe a quick reference to the woman at the well in John 4. I'm hesitant to do too much cross-referencing, but it's time to build the substance of my case.

One more thing: if you're a PowerPoint user, here's a tip. I want to always direct people to the biblical text, and my fear is that putting *too much* on the screen stops people looking at the passage in the Bible on their lap.[5] Usually, I'll put up the full text of verses I cross-reference (to save page flipping), but I'll show only the *verse reference* if it's in the main passage. You'll see that demonstrated in the next section, as I try to build a bit more tension between Israel and Samaria.

---

5   I know it's old-fashioned to talk about people "looking at the text on the page". In our church, more and more people are looking at the biblical text on the screens of their smart phones or tablets. No problem. My goal is to get people into the *flow and context* of the text, and isolated verses on the big screen are detached from that. I've also experimented with a PowerPoint format (which works quite well) that scrolls the *whole text* up and down the screen and then highlights the verses I'm talking about.

Now again, I think **we just don't get this**.

This is more than an **upstairs-downstairs thing**.

This is **generations of cultural distrust**. This is like the **Serbians** and the **Croatians**. This is **literally** like the Israelis today and the **West Bank Palestinians**.

This is a **deep-seated cultural divide** that cuts right back through Israel's history to a **civil war** when half of them broke off and set up a **rival temple**… and a **rival kingdom**. In Samaria.

Some of you diehard **Queenslanders** think you don't like **New South Wales people very much**.[6] That's **nothing**. Compared with **Israelites** and **Samaritans**.

Remember Jesus and the Samaritan woman? Remember how **John tells it**? Jesus unavoidably **has to travel through Samaria**. And he stops at a well. And asks a **Samaritan woman** for a drink. And John puts it this way… John 4 verse 9:

▶ **[SLIDE John 4:9]**

> The Samaritan woman said to him, "You are a Jew and I am a Samaritan woman. How can you ask me for a drink?" (For Jews do not associate with Samaritans.)

And they didn't.

And now here's **Philip… preaching the gospel to them**. And doing **apostle-style miracles** in front of them. And **worst of all**… **they listen**. Read from verse 5.

---

6   A note for international readers: Here in Australia there's a lighthearted state-to-state rivalry between New South Wales, in the south, and the better state, Queensland, in the north. It's not quite so lighthearted during State of Origin football season.

[SLIDE Acts 8:5]

Philip went down to a city **in Samaria** and proclaimed the Messiah there. When the crowds heard Philip and saw the signs he performed, **they all paid close attention to what he said**. For with shrieks, impure spirits came out of many, and many who were paralyzed or lame were healed. So there was great joy in that city.

See if you're a Jew, even if you're a **Jewish Christian**... this'll blow your mind—**God is at work in Samaria**. Just like he was in **Israel**. Healing cripples, driving out evil spirits. Paralyzed people walking again. And Philip's **proclaiming the Christ**—in exactly the same way. And more than that— these Samaritans are **believing**.

And in verse 12, they **believe** Philip as he preaches the good news of the kingdom and the name of Jesus Christ. And they're **baptized**.

> Here's another one of my 'top ten tips' in action. Notice, I've spent all that time building up *towards* the words "Philip went down to a city **in Samaria**" in Acts 8:5. Rather than reading the verse first and then unpacking it, I'm trying to create a sense of anticipation first. I'm working *towards the text*, rather than away from it. The same applies as I approach verse 14 and then verse 25 in the next section. I'll make the point, and then I'll show the verse.

And yet at this point, **the Spirit doesn't come on them**. Which you might be tempted to think is because these first **Samaritan Christians are somehow defective**.

See, this is no small event in the history of the church.

And are **the apostles** and the **Jerusalem church going to okay it?** Or not?

It's interesting, that's a question that's going to run all the way through Acts. Because a bit like Lord Crawley in *Downton Abbey*, they're going to be dragged **kicking and screaming** into the new era. Which we'll see most especially with **Peter next week** as God calls him to **go and eat with a Gentile**.

But for now, if you pick up in verse 14, this happens:

▶ [SLIDE Acts 8:14]

> When the apostles in Jerusalem heard that Samaria had accepted the word of God, they sent Peter and John to Samaria.

And they talk to them. And they **pray for them** that **they might receive the Holy Spirit**. These **historical enemies of Israel**. These untouchables. And then verse 17… **they touch them**. It says, "Then Peter and John **placed their hands on them**, and they **received the Holy Spirit**".

And they're **in**.

Except for poor Simon the Sorcerer who just wants to **buy a franchise** in the **Holy Spirit** without being **repentant at all**. Which just doesn't work.

And then **Peter and John**, you'll see in verse 25, head back to Jerusalem. Clearly **persuaded and converted**, you'll notice, converted to the fact that **Jesus meant business** when he said **preach to Samaria**. Clearly **persuaded** that the **Spirit** was **for Samaritans too**. Verse 25:

▶ [SLIDE Acts 8:25]

> After they had further proclaimed the word of the Lord and testified about Jesus, Peter and John returned to Jerusalem, preaching the gospel in many Samaritan villages.

And at the same time, an **angel sends Philip to the south**. Down to the Jerusalem-Gaza road that runs through the desert.

Okay. That's the first phase of the sermon. The Samaritans are baptized, they've received the Spirit, they're accepted by the apostles, and we're ready to move on to case 2: the emasculated African. Now it's time to set the scene with a look back to Isaiah 52:10 and 55:4-5, which both make the point that Isaiah foresees the day when foreigners will be welcomed with open arms because of the work of the Servant. From there, it's a short step to Isaiah 56:3. (Make sure you watch out for the kid-friendly explanation of 'eunuch' on the way!)

Now at this point can I pause and say, if the apostles had been reading their Old Testaments, none of this stuff would be surprising. If the apostles had been reading **the book of Isaiah**, they'd have been **ready**. For these **surprising new barrier-breaking friendships**. Like with the Samaritans.

Because the prophet Isaiah had mapped out **hundreds of years before** the difference that **the Messiah** was going to make. The one he said would come as a **Suffering Servant**. The one who'd be **pierced** for the **transgressions of his people**. The one, he said, who'd have the **iniquities of us all** laid **right on him**. Isaiah 53. And not just Israel's iniquities, but the nations' as well.

Because Isaiah said things like **this**:

> All the ends of the earth will see
>> the salvation of our God. (52:10)

Or this…

> "See, I have made him a witness to **the peoples**,
>> a ruler and commander of **the peoples**.
> Surely you will summon nations you know not, and
>> nations you do not know will come running to you,
> because of the LORD your God…" (55:4-5)

And Isaiah also said **this** as he **looked ahead** to this coming time of **radical change**. See, in Israel if you were a foreigner you could **come to the temple**. But only to the outer court. Kind of like if you imagine our church building here as a temple, you've got the **car park** that's the outer court, you've got the morning tea courtyard that's the inner court, then the **door**. And you're in.

In Israel if you were a foreigner… in Israel if you were **physically imperfect**… like a eunuch… in Israel if you were **unclean**. You could come to the temple. **And you'd have to stand in the car park**.

But look what Isaiah's saying. As he looks forward to the time when the **Suffering Servant messiah comes**. Because **he changes everything**.

▶ **[SLIDE Isa 56:3]**

> Let no foreigner who is bound to the LORD say,
>   "The LORD will surely exclude me from his people".
> And let no **eunuch** complain,
>   "**I am only a dry tree**".

Because Isaiah says, when that day comes, you'll be **invited in**. And it **won't just be for Israel**. But for **anyone**. Who wants to **bind themselves to the Lord**. Even if you're a **eunuch**. Or a foreigner. No matter who you are.

And guys like the apostles and like Philip should have **known that**. And probably did. But if they didn't, **Philip's about to get** a **very concrete lesson**.

Because what do you know, **here comes a foreign**… eunuch.

The **angel** says to Philip head down to the Jerusalem Gaza road. And what do you know, here's one coming now!

An Ethiopian. African. A servant in the court of Queen Candace. And a eunuch. Deliberately made to be unable to have kids. Locked into service to the royal family.

Now he's a foreigner. But he's been to Jerusalem to **worship in the temple's outer court**. Because that's as far as they'll let him in.

And now he's on his way home, **sitting in his chariot**, and he's **reading out loud from the prophet Isaiah**. And the Spirit says to Philip, verse 29, "**Go to that chariot and stay near it**".

The guy's reading Isaiah 53. The **Suffering Servant**. Led like a lamb to the slaughter.

And Philip says to him **let me explain**. Because this is great news for people **just like you**. Once excluded. Let me invite you into a whole new age. Of **sins forgiven for everyone**. Let me tell you about **Jesus**. Who invites people like you in from the **car park** not just to the courtyard but to a **seat right up the front**. Verse 35.

▶ [SLIDE Acts 8:35]

Philip begins with that **very passage of Scripture**. And tells him the good news about Jesus.

Begins there. But I'll bet you anything he doesn't stop til he gets to that bit a couple of chapters later:

> Let no foreigner who is bound to the LORD say,
> "The LORD will surely exclude me from his people".
> And let no **eunuch** complain,
> "**I am only a dry tree**".

And the eunuch says, **here's some water**. Why can't you **baptize me**? How about you **ceremonially accept me** as a

part of the church. As a subject and servant of **King Jesus**.

And so they go down into the water, verse 38, and Philip **baptizes him**; and then the **Spirit of the Lord** suddenly takes Philip away. And the eunuch… goes on his way rejoicing.

While the Spirit takes Philip on a preaching tour to **Caesarea**.

We're nearly there. We've set the scene and we've shown the link between the two major movements of the chapter, as the gospel forges unlikely friendships. As you'll notice, issues like the where, when and how of baptism have receded into the background, where in this case I think they belong. The point is: he's included. He's in—just as Isaiah had promised. All we need to do now is bring it home with some slightly more concrete application, which in this case is going to take the form of a beautiful video clip from St Albans Anglican Multicultural Bible Ministry in Rooty Hill, an outer suburb of Sydney.[7] Led by Maltese Australian Ray Galea, the church is made up of over 60 different nationalities, united by a warm common faith in Jesus. The video demonstrates the point of the passage beautifully… so my closing moves will simply set the scene for the video clip, with a final nod to the idea of 'unlikely friendships' created by the gospel.

Now here's the thing. Here's the **change of eras**.

Israel. In the Old Testament. Was all about **exclusion**. It was all about being **one nation**; especially set apart for God. And everyone else **shut outside**.

And those days are over. Because the **kingdom of Jesus is bigger than that**.

And so we're tracking the story here in Acts of how that **era of change** plays out. Samaritans. Once out. **Now in**. Ethiopians. Once in the car park. Now in the front-row seats. Eunuch. Once **barren** and **excluded**. Now enfolded. And **fruitful** in a better way.

---

7   You can take a look at the video here: www.savingeutychus.com/resources

That's something that **took a while to sink in**. In fact, right through the New Testament it runs like a **fault line**. An ongoing argument, a **debate** over whether you had to be **Jewish first** to be **really included**. A hesitation. To say and to demonstrate that **when the Spirit includes you**, then **the church should as well**. No matter where you've come from. No matter **what your social background** or your **racial background** or anything else. **Included in Christ**. As Paul puts it, **one in spirit and purpose**.

Which means church should always be a place of **unlikely friendships**. A community where you grow to know and to love people who are **most unlike you**. Because of your common bond in Jesus.

I want you to take a look at this two-minute video from a church in the west of Sydney called **Multicultural Bible Ministries**. Listen to the words. But more than that, **look at the faces**. And the **small print** at the side.

You might think it's a big thing coming to a **combined service today**. Mixing with **different people** from a **different congregation**. But have a look at the realities of life at MBM; a church made up of people from **60 different cultures**. All **loving each other**. All **united in the gospel**. In an incredible way.

And as you watch, reflect on how **we're going** here at MPC; how you're going at accepting and including anyone who's **different to you**. How you're going at **welcoming**. And incorporating. Anybody who's not quite from your background. Because if they're **okay with Jesus**… surely they should be **okay with you**. How maybe as a New Year's resolution, as a challenge for 2013, we can grow as a group of **unlikely friends**. Just like the **very first church**.

 **[PLAY VIDEO]**

So THERE IT IS. It's now Monday afternoon—the day after I preached this sermon in real life.[8] As I preached yesterday, the usual one or two nodders were looking sleepy at some points. Maybe I overplayed the scene setting, with background details both from the history of Samaria and from Isaiah. And it certainly wasn't the most lavishly illustrated sermon I've ever preached. But, on the other hand, a number of folks were visibly moved; almost everybody seemed to 'get it' and picked up on the fact that in the gospel God really is bringing all kinds of people together. Using the video clip as a finale worked beautifully. Maybe it was my imagination, but I sensed an increased warmth over morning tea, as regulars made just a little extra effort to welcome visitors and get to know one another across the boundaries of our two Sunday congregations. In the end, Alan made it all worthwhile with this comment: "I'm not sure how you did it this morning, but I've read that chapter a lot of times before, and I'd never really seen it so clearly."

Thanks, Alan. So have I—read the chapter many times. And neither had I—seen it so clearly before. But I'm glad that, this time round, we did.

8   See appendix 1 for Gary's feedback on this sermon.

Appendix 1

Real-life examples of sermon critique

So that you can see how we practise what we preach, and so you can also see how we are both still learning Sunday by Sunday, we have each reviewed a sermon by the other.[1] Here you'll find Gary's critique of the sermon Phil worked through for us in chapter 8, 'Let's build a sermon', followed by a sermon from Gary, and Phil's critique.

---

1   The feedback form we've followed, which we commend to your use, can be found in appendix 2.

a. Gary critiques Phil's sermon

Preacher's name:
Phil Campbell

Context of sermon:
Joint morning service, Mitchelton Presbyterian Church

Bible passage:
Acts 8

Title of sermon:
Unlikely Friendships

Content

Evidence of a clear **big idea** *through the sermon*
The big idea is introduced really powerfully through the *Downton Abbey* introduction, and stays centre stage all the way through.

My attention was held, and the sermon was not too long
Yes! One constant 'criticism' I have of Phil is that his sermons could go on longer (which is, let's face it, a rare complaint to level at a preacher!) but, as usual, he kept me engaged all the way through. The introduction is quite involved, but it set the sermon up so well that it was well worth using.

Short, easy to follow sentences
There isn't a wasted word in this sermon. Phil has 'perfected' the art of creating maximum impact with the minimum number of words. For example, I love the flow of this section:

> And they didn't.
> And now here's **Philip… preaching the gospel to them**.

And doing **apostle-style miracles** in front of them.
And **worst of all… they listen**.

This is typical Phil, and definitely worth copying!

Clear, easy to follow words
All the way through—he never slips into jargon or needlessly complex language.

Stories and illustrations about people
Unusually for Phil, there isn't much by way of illustration in this sermon (I think this is simply the result of having to do a fair amount of work to provide the biblical context of these events), although the *Downton Abbey* introduction and the MBM video at the end are both very definitely focused on people (both real and imaginary).

Lively narrative in present tense
There is a real sense of movement in this sermon, and a huge amount of ground is covered very efficiently. For example:

And now he's on his way home, **sitting in his chariot, and he's reading out loud from the prophet Isaiah**. And the Spirit says to Philip, verse 29, "**Go to that chariot and stay near it**".

The style felt natural and conversational
Phil does this really well—look at how naturally he expresses the following theological statements:

But **so far**… so far in the gospel accounts, so far here in the book of Acts, so far **all the action has been Jewish**.

The Spirit doesn't come on them yet. Because **the apostles** are still sitting back at Head Office in Jerusalem.

And those days are over. Because the **kingdom of Jesus is bigger than that**.

Samaritans. Once out. **Now in**. Ethiopians. Once in the car park. Now in the front-row seats.

There was repetition for clarity and emphasis
The 'upstairs, downstairs' language, the 'insider, outsider' language and the 'unlikely friends' ideas all help to carry the big idea along, constantly reminding listeners of where we are going.

Sometimes even obvious things were illustrated
The conclusion is a great example of how this works. The video doesn't really say anything new, but it 'puts flesh' on the big idea.

When we looked directly at a Bible verse, my interest had already been raised
Phil does this all the way through—his first example illustrates the power of using this approach:

And at last, here at the start of chapter 8, **it changes**. For the **most unlikely reason**. We're picking up right after the **stoning of Stephen**. And look what happens… chapter 8 verse 1.

On that day a great persecution broke out against the church in Jerusalem, and **all except the apostles** were scattered **throughout Judea and Samaria**.

Delivery

Variation in pitch
Phil doesn't think he does, but he does vary his pitch considerably!

Variation in volume
Lots.

Variation in pace
Phil does this easily and naturally.

There was energy and interest in the way the sermon was delivered
Oh yes!

Can you summarize the main idea of the sermon?
That God's plan to unite Jew and Gentile in Christ by the Spirit has been fulfilled, and so we are now in this together!

Duration

How long was the sermon?
22 minutes

Did it feel too long? (Please be honest!)
No. As I said above, I think Phil could have spoken for at least another five minutes.

Application

Did this message move you to change anything in your thinking or life?
The MBM video is really powerful, and I was moved when I saw it for the first time. I have no doubt that it will have

made a real impact on many people in the church family. I do just wonder if it may have left people the option of thinking, "Isn't it lovely that this happens there" rather than examining their own hearts and thinking through what God asks of us at MPC. I think it would have been helpful to spend a few extra minutes fleshing out the implications for MPC, and the particular challenges we face in our context. At the end, the video encouraged us to come and partner in 'their' vision— might it have been useful to put some flesh on what *our* vision is? Some more 'heart' stuff on why we react so sinfully against other people who are not like us (and who those people might be) would have been really helpful.

Was Jesus Christ central to the ideas and application of this sermon?
Definitely.

Were the application points shaped by a clear understanding of the gospel?
Yes. Clearly.

General comments
How could this sermon have been improved?
This was a fantastic explanation of Acts 8, and Phil set it so helpfully in the context of the whole book. I'm with Alan on that—Phil opened up the chapter in a really fresh and helpful way. Perhaps it would have helped sharpen the sermon even more to get to the application earlier rather than leaving it all to the end, and then to use the video to set up a final couple of minutes of application to MPC.

Linking the incidents in Acts 8, and making it clear that they belong together, was very helpful. The sermon felt thoroughly integrated, and each bit played an important part in the whole. I did wonder if at points there was too much background and not enough time spent on the text itself. We had Acts 1, Isaiah, John 4 as well as the passage at hand. Having said that, though, I'm not sure which I would have left out. It just felt like it was quite a lot of additional information to take on board in addition to the colourful events of Acts 8.

Are there any other thoughts you'd like to share?
I love the way Phil handled the role of the apostles in Samaria—I have never heard that done with such a light touch.

A final note from Phil

When Englishman Simon Cowell burst on the scene as a judge on *American Idol*, contestants were shocked at the sometimes brutal frankness of his remarks. Gen-Y kids are used to being showered with praise and they have shelves stacked with trophies and awards 'just for turning up'. Gary's comments on my sample sermon are pretty gentle (partly because he didn't want to crush his co-author in print!). Some Sundays when I've preached with Gary in the congregation his feedback hasn't been quite so positive! It's painful at the time, but incredibly helpful. For years I met annually with a group of preaching friends, and we'd all bring a recording of a sermon to critique together. It was robust. I was most regularly pushed on whether I'd really cracked the 'big idea', whether I'd failed to remove some dull bits, and whether I could have pushed further and deeper with application. I often felt I'd just gone five rounds with Simon Cowell. But it was incredibly helpful. And I'm still working at improving in all those areas.

b. A sermon from Gary

Acts 3:1-4:12: Life in a Changed World[2]

Introduction

There are moments in all of our lives which we really can say change things forever. So for example, the day we got married, and the day each of our kids were born, and the day we got on a plane for Australia all had a massive, life-changing impact on Fiona and me. However, I would be very surprised if the 11th July 1992, 2nd June 2001, 18th December 2002, 22nd September 2006 and 3rd January 2012 hold nearly as much significance for you as they do for our family!

But there are moments in history that are so significant, they really do affect all of us—whatever age we are, wherever we're living at the time, and whatever we are doing with our lives. There are some moments when the world changes for good. Other moments like 28th July 1914, or 21st July 1969 or 11th September 2001. These were significant moments when the world really did change.

And that's what happened when Jesus Christ came to earth, died, beat death, returned to his Father and poured out the Spirit. We can't put a date on it. Lots of people didn't realize how unbelievably important all this was. But it changed everything. And that's what these chapters are all about. Luke carefully explains for us that the events he has carefully related in his Gospel and the first two chapters of Acts have changed the world forever. The first sign of that comes in Acts 3.

---

2   I (Gary) preached this sermon at Mitchelton Presbyterian Church, Brisbane, on 2 December 2012. If you'd like to listen to the sermon, you can find the audio and a video here: www.savingeutychus.com/resources. The style of my written manuscript differs from Phil's (in addition to scripting my sermon so that I sound like myself!). I usually put the biblical text in italics, and the subheadings are for me to mark the progression in the argument (the script itself has the verbal transitions).

According to Luke, this 'very normal miracle'—the healing of a lame man at the Jewish temple in Jerusalem—*is a sign that the world has changed.*

A very normal miracle? (3:1-10)[3]

Luke tells us exactly what happened in 3:1-10. It's a great story—the unknowing beggar looks for money, and Peter comes up with the brilliant line in verse 6, *"Silver or gold I do not have, but what I do have I give you. In the name of Jesus Christ of Nazareth, walk"*. And he did. The man was instantly, dramatically and permanently healed. The sight of him jumping around like a lunatic in the temple square must have made quite an impact! It's not surprising that Luke says in verse 10 that everyone was *"filled with wonder and amazement at what had happened to him"*.

Now at first glance, this does just look like a pretty standard miracle—there are loads of them in the gospels, and, on the face of it, this looks like more of the same. If a miracle can ever be 'ordinary', then this is an ordinary miracle. A bloke who can't walk. One sentence is spoken, and now he can. It actually seems quite matter-of-fact.

Except for one little detail. And this detail actually unlocks the whole of Acts 3 and 4 for us. Peter and John don't heal this man with their own power. They don't even pray and then do it. They say, *"In the name of Jesus Christ of Nazareth, walk!"* So how is the man healed? Not because Peter and John know the magic words, *but because Jesus is openly acknowledged as the only source of help and salvation.* Jesus is there. He is at work. The healing is all down to him. The only power here belongs to Jesus. Peter and John point this out over and over again in these chapters. *Jesus may be gone, but he is still healing people!*

---

3   All Scripture quotations in this sermon are from the New International Version (2011 edition).

I'm not sure how much you know about Knut, son of Forkbeard, son of Harald, son of Gorm the Old. If I told you that he was King of Denmark, Norway, parts of Sweden as well as England in the 11th century, you may still be none the wiser, but if I said that his name is sometimes pronounced Canute, then something to do with sitting in the sea commanding it to stop might stir somewhere in the back of your mind. Now I always thought that Canute had got a bit carried away with himself, thinking he really could tell the sea to stop. But actually the opposite is true. King Knut was actually a pretty godly king, and got so fed up with the flattery of his courtiers that he moved his throne onto the beach, commanded the waves not to wet his feet and then jumped up and shouted, *Let all men know how empty and worthless is the power of kings, for there is none worthy of the name, but He whom heaven, earth, and sea obey by eternal laws.* He then hung his gold crown on a stick and never wore it again. That's the point of this miracle. Real power can only be found in one person—the risen, ruling Jesus Christ, whom Peter and John acknowledge as the only one who can help this man.

Not surprisingly, people come running from every part of the temple complex to see what is going on (verse 11). Then Peter starts to talk. And as he talks, he explains that there has been a huge change in the way that people like us can relate to God. And that change is centred on a man called Jesus of Nazareth. Verse 16 is the key verse here—this is what it says:

> By faith in the name of Jesus, this man whom you see and know was made strong. It is Jesus' name and the faith that comes through him that has completely healed him, as you can all see.

Again, the focus falls on the name of Jesus.

At this point, it helps to know that in the first part of the

Bible, the Old Testament, over and over again, people are told to *call on the name of the Lord*. You can see that, for example, if you turn back just one page to 2:21 on page 1903, where Peter quotes the prophet Joel saying, *"everyone who calls on the name of the Lord will be saved"*. Now, however, it seems that rescue, healing, even forgiveness is available to people *who call on the name of Jesus*. Now that's a big shock!

Just before we left Ireland, I went to the dentist. And I got a shock. For almost 40 years, I had been going to the same dentist. Phil, as he is appropriately called, was not only our dentist, but lived three doors down. He was also an elder in my home church. And he was an excellent dentist. However, Phil the Dentist rather inconsiderately retired last September. Some young whippersnapper who looks about 30 had taken his place. Now for the first time in years, I felt slightly apprehensive at the dentist. Even though the surgery hadn't moved, even though I was sitting in the same chair in the same room, it felt very, very odd to see a new face behind the mask!

It must have been so strange to hear Peter say that from now on, rather than calling on the name of the Lord, we are to call on the name of the Lord Jesus Christ. God has introduced Jesus to us as the one who has now taken on the role of bringing people like us to know God. God has made it so clear that Jesus is the Messiah, the promised King, the one who makes it possible for us to live with God—so from now on, if we want to know God, we call on him. God has set up a new way of relating to him—a new covenant, to use the Bible's word—this is broadband access to God. And at the centre of this huge change in the way religion works is Jesus himself.

This 'run of the mill' miracle actually *signals that the world has changed*. There has been a seismic shift in the way people like us can relate to God. Jesus himself performed this miracle through his followers. He is the one we are to call on. Because of his coming to earth, and death and resurrection, and ascension, and gift of the Spirit. *The world has changed.* In the rest of our passage, Luke spells out what difference this actually makes—first, in the life of one changed man, and then in the way we all think about our world.

A changed man (3:11-26)

As we read through Acts 3 and 4, it becomes clear that Peter, the leader of Jesus' followers, is a changed man. The speech on the Day of Pentecost in Acts 2 wasn't just a flash in the pan; he really has changed. For a start, he has a really clear grip on the fact that Jesus' coming fulfils the whole of the Bible so far.

Peter's argument is detailed but it isn't complicated. Basically what he does is point out how God has made it clear that Jesus of Nazareth is the one who is anticipated in all the key parts of the Old Testament

He is the Servant of the Lord promised by the prophet Isaiah—you can see that in verse 13: "*The God of Abraham, Isaac and Jacob, the God of our fathers, has glorified his servant Jesus.*" Peter's language suggests he's not just talking about any old servant, but *the* servant, the Servant with a capital S who comes to suffer and die in our place. But that's not all.

He is the king who reigns forever anticipated by King David. Even though the people of Jerusalem *"disowned the Holy and Righteous One"* and *"killed the author of life… God raised him from the dead"* God has made it abundantly clear that Jesus is the descendant of David who, it was said, would set up a kingdom that lasts forever. If you're going to do that, beating death is actually a prerequisite, and that's what Jesus did.

He is also the 'prophet like me' who Moses said would come. That's spelled out in verses 22-23. References don't come any better than that, so God's people really should have listened to him.

He is the descendant of Abraham promised in Genesis. Right at the start of the Bible, God had said that he would bless the whole world through one of Abraham's family. In verse 25, Peter says "Yes, that's Jesus too!"

So Peter said to that stampeding crowd in the temple: *Jesus Christ did this. Not only is he alive and at work, he is the one Abraham talked about right at the start of our nation; he's the one Moses talked about as we made it into the Promised Land; he's the one King David talked about at his own coronation, when he said a much greater king was coming; he's the one Isaiah talked about when he said that even though we wander off like sheep, someone is coming to pay for all our stupidity. In fact (verse 24), the whole Bible has been talking about him. And now he has come.* **The world has changed**, because Jesus the Messiah has come. And that explains the **dramatic change in the apostle Peter**.

Up to this point, Peter didn't have a great track record when it came to answering theological questions. Every time Jesus asked him one, he mucked it up. Just a few pages earlier, in the gospels, Peter had basically told Jesus not to be so stupid when he said he was going to die on a cross. On the night before Jesus died, Peter was put on the spot outside the makeshift courtyard. Someone said, "You were with Jesus, weren't you?" And Peter gave a brilliant explanation of all that he had heard and seen. Well actually, no he didn't. He said, "No I wasn't, and I'll thump you if you say that again". So what's the difference? He is a changed man.

This is the religious equivalent of Michelle Smith. You may not have heard of Michelle Smith. But she is Ireland's most famous Olympic medal-winning swimmer—actually, she's Ireland's only Olympic medal-winning swimmer. Mysteriously, in the run-up to the Atlanta games in 1996 she went from utter obscurity to winning three gold medals and a bronze in a matter of months. Even now no-one knows how, or whether she cheated. She was banned for tampering with a urine sample but that was two years after the games, so she still has her medals, and is Ireland's greatest ever Olympian by some distance. What no-one can dispute is that almost overnight, she went from mediocrity to being one of the fastest swimmers in the world. Peter's transformation into this brave and brilliant speaker is just as impressive. So what changed?

First of all, this—page 1062—*Luke 24:44-48:* The risen Jesus shows up for dinner. But he isn't just there for the food. He teaches them:

> *He said to them, "This is what I told you while I was still with you: Everything must be fulfilled that is written about me in the Law of Moses, the Prophets and the Psalms."*
>
> *Then he opened their minds so they could understand the Scriptures. He told them, "This is what is written: The Messiah will suffer and rise from the dead on the third day, and repentance for the forgiveness of sins will be preached in his name to all nations, beginning at Jerusalem."*

The first step in Peter's transformation is that Jesus teaches him Old Testament 101. And then, of course, God pours out his Spirit on Peter and his friends. The difference in Peter is that he's now understood the message of the Bible, and he has the Spirit. The two always go hand in hand. This is how *God changes people* like you and me.

And isn't this exactly what we have going for us? If we belong to Jesus, then we have the Spirit, and we have the Bible and people to explain it to us. This is what changes lives. This is what equips us, not to be the apostle Peter, but to be witnesses, as we were looking at a couple of weeks ago. I know you probably feel weak and inadequate. Most of us feel like that most of the time. Especially, I suspect, when it comes to talking about Jesus. But we have God's own words, and we have God's Spirit.

Think about that! I don't know if you usually think of yourself like this—but if you have handed control over to the Lord Jesus, then you should. You are someone in whom the Spirit of the Lord Jesus Christ lives. We are not alone. We are not powerless. We are not trapped. We are not destined to be failures. We are people who have already been changed and are being changed by the Spirit. And how does the Spirit change us? The Spirit takes the message of Jesus, helps us to grasp it, and works it deep into our thinking, and our longing, and our deciding, so that we becoming increasingly like Jesus, the one whose Spirit lives in us. This is who we are.

So a blind man is healed through the name of Jesus, and Peter, a changed man, explains the significance of what has just happened. But remember these chapters are about more than Peter being changed—the world has changed because Jesus the Messiah has showed up. This has huge implications, which becomes clear when we look on to chapter 4. Chapter 4 is a picture of life in a changed world.

Life in a changed world
When they hear Peter speak, another couple of thousand become followers of Jesus and join the church family in Jerusalem (4:4). This, however, was seen as a problem by the religious hierarchy. So all the great and the good put their heads together, and tried to work out how to put a stop to this nonsense. They dragged Peter and John in, and tried to put the frighteners on them. But needless to say it didn't work. Why

not? *Because they were changed men living in a changed world.*

In the speech that Peter makes to the leaders of his nation he says two things which sum up why all this stuff about Jesus being the Messiah really matters, and why Jesus' coming has changed the world forever. Here are two key facts which hold the key to living in this changed world—our world, the world after Jesus has come.

Salvation is only found in Jesus Christ (4:12)

The first is found in 4:12 but Peter builds up to it from verse 8, when he is asked "By what power or what name did you do this?" Peter doesn't miss his cue, and says, *"Know this, you and all the people of Israel: It is by the name of Jesus Christ of Nazareth, whom you crucified but whom God raised from the dead, that this man stands before you healed"*. Remember that Peter is standing in front of the equivalent of Julia Gillard and the Cabinet as he says this. He spells it out for them in way that they really couldn't misunderstand. Verse 12 says, *"Salvation is found in no-one else, for there is no other name under heaven given to mankind by which we must be saved"*. It seems there was a long silence when Peter said that. The ruling council could see the implications of his claim. We need to make sure that we're clear on this too—for this is the way it is in our world.

Acts 4:12 says that the only way to know God, to be rescued by God and to enjoy God forever is through Jesus Christ. At least 5 things follow…

1. All religions are not the same—or to put it another way, Christianity and all other world faiths are contradictory and incompatible. Either Christianity is true, or it isn't. That's why you can't be a Christian Buddhist. That's like saying you are a vegan who likes nothing better than a bacon sandwich.
2. All religions do not lead to God. If Acts 4:12 is true, then

by definition all other religions ultimately do not deliver. That's not to say that they don't say some helpful things, or that everyone who follows them is a horrible person, but if Jesus is the only name under heaven by which we can be rescued, then people who are calling on other names are barking up the wrong tree. That's tragic, and dangerous.

3. We need to be rescued. If Acts 4:12 is true, then everyone who is not a Christian is still in grave danger, and needs to be rescued.

4. Sincerity (or belief or spirituality or being religious) is not enough. The strength of our feelings, or depth of our piety, or frequency of our practice cannot rescue us. Only Jesus can. Trusting in Jesus' name—that is, in who he is and what he has done for us—is the only way to be safe and to be free.

5. As followers of Jesus, we will always be out of step with society. One of the interesting things about the world in which Jesus lived was that it was extremely 'pluralistic'— that is, there were more religions on offer than you could shake a stick at. Isn't it exactly the same for us? We now live in a world where to say anything critical about another person's lifestyle or moral convictions is almost unforgivable—unless they are either a politician or an orthodox Christian. That means if we believe Acts 4:12 to be true, then we won't win any popularity contests.

If Jesus is who he claims to be, and who the Bible says he is, it does and will matter, because it means that life and freedom and joy—salvation—is to be found in no-one else. This is the way it is in our changed world.

We should obey God, not other people

The other reason it matters is that if this is true, if God really has intervened in our world through Jesus Christ, if he made us, and loves us, and has our destiny in his hands, *then we really do need to obey HIM and not other people*. Which is why Peter and John say what they do in verses 19-20. When offered their freedom conditional on shutting up about Jesus, *"Peter and John replied, 'Which is right in God's eyes: to listen to you, or to him? You be the judges! As for us, we cannot help speaking about what we have seen and heard.'"* Peter and John realized that because God is God, and has acted for our good and his glory in Jesus, then it would be utterly stupid to listen to these twisted, self-serving human leaders rather than God himself.

It's important to notice that for Peter and John this wasn't a particularly admirable quality. It isn't that they have such courage, or such devotion, or such strength that they can choose to follow God. For them, it was the only option that made any sense at all.

Sometimes, from my perspective, our girls make poor decisions. Sometimes, they listen to their friends rather than listening to their parents. Then we get the age-old excuse, "But _____ told me to do it". Now when I was seven or nine, this seemed to me like a very reasonable excuse. My friend told me to do it. I wanted to please my friend, and not to look stupid in front of her, so I did what she said. But from where I am standing now, this looks like pretty weak reasoning. I mean, who are you going to listen to? Someone from your class who is also seven, who is going home in 20 minutes and who may not still be your friend tomorrow, or your dad? It's a no-brainer. And yet kids constantly make the wrong choice.

Peter makes it really clear for us that once we realize who Jesus is and what he has done, once we realize that the world has changed, then choosing to please other people rather than God is just plain stupid. Now that's a hard one for us—because most of us are, at some level, people-pleasers. We want to keep the people we care about happy. So we'll tell them what they want to hear. We'll do what they want us to do. At times, we'll even be the people they want us to be. Why? Because like children, we have slipped into living to please our friends, rather than pleasing God. So what are we to do?

We need to ask God to work the fact that Jesus Christ is Lord and that salvation is found in him alone a little deeper into our heads and hearts. We have the Spirit, and we have the message of Jesus, who has changed the world. In one sense, we don't need anything new. We certainly don't need anything more. We simply need God to change our minds, to bring us into line with the truth, to help us to see the world through his eyes, through the lens of the gospel. We need to ask God to help us to believe what we already know. We need to exercise faith—we need to trust Jesus, and live to please him, rather than ourselves or other people.

Conclusion

So here's the message of this long section: everything has changed—now that Jesus has died and risen, we need to call on *his* name, and nobody else's, because nobody else can deliver. Only he is our King, so the only sensible thing to do is entrust ourselves to him. Which is exactly what Peter says in 3:19-20, and with this I'll stop: *"Repent, then, and turn to God, so that your sins may be wiped out, that times of refreshing may come from the Lord, and that he may send the Messiah, who has been appointed for you—even Jesus."*

To repent is to face the fact we've mucked up, turn back to God and to start to do what he tells us. So whether we've been living to please other people, or wimping out of talking about Jesus, or acting like we're too weak to live for Jesus, or just been struggling along without any sense of the fact that

God lives in us by his Spirit, this is what we need to do. Face it, turn back to God, and remember that Jesus is Lord and his Spirit lives in us.

And why should we do it? Peter says we should do it so that our sins may be wiped out—so that we can feel clean on the inside, and we don't have to carry around all our past guilt. So that we don't have to lug around the guilt of all our past mistakes. So that we're not dragged down by our past failures. Peter says we should come back to God so that we might enjoy times of refreshing from God. Of course, life isn't perfect, but it is so much better when we are actually living it with and for God. And Peter says we should repent so that we get to enjoy God's forever happiness in the new creation. I can't think where else we are going to find freedom from the past, freedom to enjoy the messy present, and the prospect of a perfect future, can you?

And this all flows from the fact that one random lame man was healed with one sentence. That simple—and yet incredibly powerful—act made it very clear that the world had changed. Everything had changed. For Jesus had come. Jesus is Lord. Jesus is at work in our world. Salvation belongs to him. Obeying him is the only thing that makes sense. This is reality. This is the truth. Let's ask God to give us grace to recognize it, and live in a way that shows that we know that Jesus has changed the world.

c. Phil critiques Gary's sermon

Preacher's name:
Gary Millar

Context of sermon:
Morning services, Mitchelton Presbyterian Church

Bible passage:
Acts 3:1-4:12

Title of sermon:
Life in a Changed World

Content

Evidence of a clear big idea *through the sermon*
By the time we get to the end of the introduction, we get it!
The idea of change then works its way all the way through the
sermon.

My attention was held, and the sermon was not too long
Yes. Very easy to stay tuned in, due to the pace and movement.

Short, easy to follow sentences
Gary has perfected the style of scripting his sermon in a
way that sounds exactly like him! His sentence lengths and
rhythms are different to mine, and his speaking style is slightly
more formal. That's exactly as it should be, because that's the
way you'll find us to be if you chat with us in the car park. Even
so, notice the number of short, punchy sentences, like "Except
for one little detail" and "Jesus is there."

Clear, easy to follow words

Although Gary has a tendency to be "apprehensive" at the dentist when I'm more likely to be "scared out of my wits" or to save five letters with a simpler "nervous"—and while he'll occasionally drop a "whilst" into the mix, while I'm all for "while"—the words he chooses are simple and clear. More importantly, they're exactly the same words he'd use in a normal conversation.

Stories and illustrations about **people**

Absolutely. Every time! (Even if it is an obscure Norse king that nobody has heard of, or an equally obscure Irish swimmer!)

Lively narrative in **present tense**

Gary immediately (and instinctively) switches into present tense as he retells narrative. The beggar "*looks* for money", and Peter "*comes up* with the brilliant line". We're there! I'd probably push it a bit further though—Gary reverts to past tense with "And he *did*". Why not keep it live with "And he *does*!"? But as Gary preaches this, his style is so animated that the excitement of the event is contagious anyway.

The style felt natural and conversational

Completely.

There was repetition for clarity and emphasis

We've grabbed hold of the idea that this is going to be a sermon about world-changing events! Did you notice how many times Gary repeats the word 'change' in the introduction? Seven times! And it's no small change we're talking about—"change things forever", "life-changing impact", "world changes for good", "the world really did change", "changed everything", "changed the world forever", "a sign that the world has changed".

Sometimes even obvious things were illustrated
Yes. The Michelle Smith story was simply illustrating the idea of 'surprising change'. It wasn't a complex point that needed explaining—just a great story, at just the right time to be refreshing.

When we looked directly at a Bible verse, my interest had already been raised
A good example of this is at the start of the conclusion, where Gary pre-states his point, then nails it with the text of 3:19-20. Look again:

> So here's the message of this long section: everything has changed—now that Jesus has died and risen, we need to call on *his* name, and nobody else's, because nobody else can deliver. Only he is our King, so the only sensible thing to do is entrust ourselves to him. Which is exactly what Peter says in 3:19-20, and with this I'll stop: "*Repent, then, and turn to God, so that your sins may be wiped out, that times of refreshing may come from the Lord, and that he may send the Messiah, who has been appointed for you—even Jesus.*"

Delivery

Variation in pitch
As an Irishman with a lilting accent, Gary's variation in pitch is natural and beautifully engaging, and it makes me feel like a dull monotone Aussie. (Oh. I am? Sorry.)

Variation in volume
Plenty.

Variation in pace
Nice energetic average pace, with plenty of variation.

There was energy and interest in the way the sermon was delivered
Absolutely.

Can you summarize the main idea of the sermon?
The world has been dramatically changed, as now we come to God through the name of Jesus and are changed by the word and the Spirit to serve not in our own strength but his.

Duration
How long was the sermon?
28 minutes

Did it feel too long? (Please be honest!)
I prefer 23 minutes, but Gary held me all the way through. That's because he's good at it!

Application
Did this message move you to change anything in your thinking or life?
There was a lot of application! This is one of the areas where our styles are a bit different—Gary applies everything that can possibly flow from the main point, and I tend to be a bit more focused. The five implications of the fact that there's "no other name under heaven given to mankind by which we must be saved" were really strong. But then maybe I would have built the whole sermon (and reshaped the introduction, etc.) as a lead-up to this. Then perhaps the 'name of Jesus' would have been the integrating thread through the passage.

Having said that, the 'repent and be refreshed' section was… refreshing. It's always great to be reminded that it's not up to me!

Was Jesus Christ central to the ideas and application of this sermon?
Absolutely. The *name of Jesus* was at the heart of everything. (Maybe this was an easy passage to do that from!)

Were the application points shaped by a clear understanding of the gospel?
Yes—explicitly so.

General comments

How could this sermon have been improved?
There's one small thing I'd do differently in the opening—drop the dates! Sure, they add interesting detail, but it's then awkward to come to the really big events of Jesus and have to say, "We can't put a date on it". It's as if we've been built up towards some climactic 'dates' but then have to change gears. It's just a small detail. But it could be a momentary distraction for people listening.

Also, I'd be careful with the assumption that everyone has heard of King Canute. Unfortunately, nothing was stirring in the back of my mind when Gary thought it should be. We don't want to make people feel under-educated!

Are there any other thoughts you'd like to share?
The way Gary condensed Peter's long and complex speech was very skilful. Some preachers would take half an hour to unpack that stuff. It's certainly worth looking at in detail, but that's probably better done in a small group or as a sermon on

its own. In this case, it's a really helpful summary and keeps us going with the flow of the big idea of 'change'. (I sometimes think the art of summary is a key preaching skill—and Gary demonstrated it here!)

A final note from Gary

Over the years, I've had my fair share of critique that was much more painful than Phil's on this sermon! Insightful feedback in several key areas has really helped my preaching. My mistakes and weaknesses have included:

- getting the big idea (spectacularly) wrong
- using too many illustrations about myself
- trying to sound like someone else
- being self-indulgent (by including material that fascinated me but wasn't any help to people in living for Jesus)
- being unclear—either in particular sections or, worse (because it's much harder to fix), in the overall argument, flow or structure
- failing to apply the text to people's hearts
- saying stuff that was just plain wrong (or at best highly misleading).

I'm grateful for, and humbled by, the opportunities I've had (and continue to have) to work on these areas. It seems self-evident that we can all greatly benefit from feedback on our preaching.

Appendix 2
Resources

a. Sermon feedback form

Here is the feedback form we use for sermon critique at Queensland Theological College—it's the one we both used to critique each other's sermons in appendix 1. When QTC students preach in their home churches, we ask them to request that a number of select listeners fill out this sheet. We encourage you to use this form as you ask for, and offer, regular, godly feedback on your preaching.

Preacher's name:

Context of sermon:
(e.g. in church, youth group, dinner, etc.)

Bible passage:

Title of sermon:

Please rate the following Yes/Maybe/No:

Content

Evidence of a clear big idea *through the sermon*

My attention was held, and the sermon was not too long

Short, easy to follow sentences

Clear, easy to follow words

Stories and illustrations about people

Lively narrative in present tense

The style felt natural and conversational

There was repetition for clarity and emphasis

Sometimes even obvious things were illustrated

When we looked directly at a Bible verse, my interest had already been raised

Delivery

Variation in pitch

Variation in volume

Variation in pace

There was energy and interest in the way the sermon was delivered

Can you summarize the main idea of the sermon?

Duration

How long was the sermon?

Did it feel too long? (Please be honest!)

Application

Did this message move you to change anything in your thinking or life?

Was Jesus Christ central to the ideas and application of this sermon?

Were the application points shaped by a clear understanding of the gospel?

General comments

How could this sermon have been improved?

Are there any other thoughts you'd like to share?

b. Phil's top ten tips checklist

Run through this list quickly before you start your sermon preparation each week, and then again as you finalize what you're going to say.

1. The more you say, the less people will remember ☐

2. Make the 'big idea' shape everything you say ☐

3. Choose the shortest, most ordinary words you can ☐

4. Use shorter sentences ☐

5. Forget everything your English teacher taught you ☐
   And boldly start sentences with conjunctions. Contract. And no complex clauses!

6. Repeat yourself ☐
   Repeat yourself.

7. Translate narratives into the present tense ☐

8. Illustrate the obvious ☐

9. Talk about real people ☐

10. Work towards your key text ☐
    Explain and *then* show your Bible verse(s).

c. Dynamic delivery diagram worksheet

Make a copy of this page, grab someone who's willing to listen to you, and ask them to plot the line they hear as you deliver a sermon. (It's kind of tricky to draw a 3D plot on a piece of paper, so they'll need to use their imagination… but they'll soon get the idea.) Abandon your natural embarrassment and challenge your listener to travel to the outer reaches of the margins!

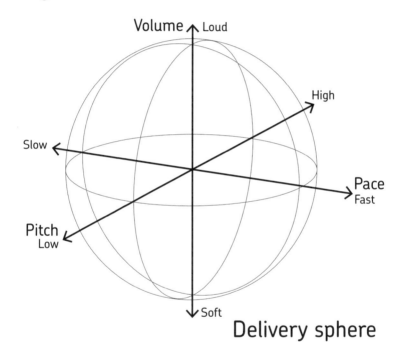

Delivery sphere

Afterword

WHAT, THEN, CAN WE SAY? Pray. Preach gospel-centred sermons from your heart to change hearts. Pray. Wrestle with God's word until you have a big idea that faithfully communicates the message of the passage, and then craft a sermon that communicates and applies that idea clearly and winsomely. Pray. Apply the message to yourself. Pray. Preach the gospel from everywhere in the Bible. Pray. Deliver your message with the energy and passion that only God can give you. Push yourself out of your comfort zone. Pray. Seek and receive critique on your preaching. Pray some more. Preach. Pray. Repeat.

That's all.

matthiasmedia

Matthias Media is an evangelical publishing ministry that seeks to persuade all Christians of the truth of God's purposes in Jesus Christ as revealed in the Bible, and equip them with high-quality resources, so that by the work of the Holy Spirit they will:

- abandon their lives to the honour and service of Christ in daily holiness and decision-making
- pray constantly in Christ's name for the fruitfulness and growth of his gospel
- speak the Bible's life-changing word whenever and however they can— in the home, in the world and in the fellowship of his people.

It was in 1988 that we first started pursuing this mission, and in God's kindness we now have more than 300 different ministry resources being used all over the world. These resources range from Bible studies and books through to training courses and audio sermons.

To find out more about our large range of very useful resources, and to access samples and free downloads, visit our website:

www.matthiasmedia.com

How to buy our resources

1. Direct from us over the internet:
  – in the US: www.matthiasmedia.com
  – in Australia and the rest of the world: www.matthiasmedia.com.au

2. Direct from us by phone:
  – in the US: 1 866 407 4530
  – in Australia: 1300 051 220
  – international: +61 2 9233 4627

> Register at our website for our **free** regular email update to receive information about the latest new resources **exclusive special offers**, and free articles to help you grow in your Christian life and ministry.

3. Through a range of outlets in various parts of the world. Visit **www.matthiasmedia.com/contact** for details about recommended retailers in your part of the world, including www.thegoodbook.co.uk in the United Kingdom.

4. Trade enquiries can be addressed to:
  – in the US and Canada: sales@matthiasmedia.com
  – in Australia and the rest of the world: sales@matthiasmedia.com.au